The Complete
Nail Technician

Hairdressing And Beauty Industry Authority series – related titles

Hairdressing

Start Hairdressing: The Official Guide to Level 1 by Martin Green and Leo Palladino

Hairdressing – The Foundations: The Official Guide to Level 2 by Leo Palladino

Professional Hairdressing: The Official Guide to Level 3 by Martin Green, Lesley Kimber and Leo Palladino

Men's Hairdressing: Traditional and Modern Barbering by Maurice Lister

African-Caribbean Hairdressing by Sandra Gittens

The World of Hair: A Scientific Companion by Dr John Gray

Salon Management by Martin Green

Mahogany Hairdressing: Steps to Cutting, Colouring and Finishing Hair by Martin Gannon and Richard Thompson

Mahogany Hairdressing: Advanced Looks by Martin Gannon and Richard Thompson (publishing October 2001)

Patrick Cameron: Dressing Long Hair by Patrick Cameron and Jacki Wadeson

Patrick Cameron: Dressing Long Hair Book 2 by Patrick Cameron

Bridal Hair by Pat Dixon and Jacki Wadeson

Trevor Sorbie: Visions in Hair by Kris Sorbie and Jacki Wadeson

The Total Look: The Style Guide for Hair and Make-up Professionals by Ian Mistlin

Art of Hair Colouring by David Adams and Jacki Wadeson

Beauty Therapy

Beauty Therapy – The Foundations: The Official Guide to Level 2 by Lorraine Nordmann

Professional Beauty Therapy: The Official Guide to Level 3 by Lorraine Nordmann, Lorraine Appleyard and Pamela Linforth

Aromatherapy for the Beauty Therapist by Valerie Ann Worwood

The World of Skin Care: A Scientific Companion by Dr John Gray

Indian Head Massage by Muriel Burnham-Airey and Adele O'Keefe

Safety in the Salon by Elaine Almond

The Complete Nail Technician: A Handbook for Artificial Nail Professionals by Marian Newman

The Complete Nail Technician

A Handbook for Artificial Nail Professionals

MARIAN NEWMAN

HABIA
Hairdressing And Beauty Industry Authority

THOMSON
LEARNING

Australia · Canada · Mexico · Singapore · Spain · United Kingdom · United States

The Complete Nail Technician: A Handbook for Artificial Nail Professionals

British Library Cataloguing-in-Publication Data
A catalogue record for this book is available from the British Library

ISBN 1-86152-723-3

First edition 2001 Thomson Learning

Typeset by Meridian Colour Repro Ltd, Pangbourne-on-Thames, Berkshire
Printed in Italy by G. Canale & C.

Contents

Foreword

When I arrived at HABIA in 1995 I knew very little about the nail industry. I wanted to familiarise myself with this aspect of the beauty service industry, so I asked around. The name to which everyone referred was that of Marian Newman.

Our first meeting left me with a strong sense of her direction, knowledge and presence within the profession. Marian talked, with great clarity, on the structure and history of the nail industry, offering information and valuable tips. One such tip was the need for a book covering the UK standards for nail technicians. I asked her to write it for us.

This book epitomises that first conversation. Covering the National Occupation Standards, it is packed with useful information and handy tips for beginners and professionals alike. It's a first for HABIA and for Thomson Learning. I hope it's a first for you!

Alan Goldsboro
Chief Executive Officer
Hairdressing And Beauty Industry Authority

Acknowledgements

The author and publishers would like to thank the following people and organisations for their assistance in producing this book:

United Beauty Products Ltd
Beauty Express
Grafton International
Debbie Timberlake
Jane Newton
Tina Rooke

The author would specially like to thank Stuart Dickinson for his continued support, encouragement and belief in 'the vision'; Electra Sawbridge for her understanding in what I wanted to do; Kay Dodd for starting it all with me; Nick Knight for being the best and quietly appreciating what I can do.

And, far from least, a very long suffering husband, Malcolm, who has always trusted, believed and supported me in everything I choose to do.

The Complete Nail Technician
About this book

The Complete Nail Technician is a book written by a technician for technicians. It provides all the necessary information for those just starting to learn the skill and also provides a 'one stop shop' for experienced technicians in a vast range of generic information that is often hard to find as most information is produced by product companies and specifically relates to their products.

All the **National Occupational Standards** requirements are included but are broken down into a natural progression of learning and reinforcement. If the book is followed in sequence, the learner will become a proficient technician. The experienced technician will be able to look up invaluable information and facts.

The UK has not had a textbook that concentrates solely on artificial nails, in all the aspects of what is a very wide subject. The book concentrates on the artificial substances and products that need to be applied to the natural nail, the care of nail and skin, the implications of using the products and chemicals involved and the potential effects for both client and technician. There are many very good books available that provide all the necessary information on manicures and natural nail treatments. This aspect is not included in this book but it does approach the subject of artificial nails in its entirety while stressing the importance of manicure as a treatment option for every client.

The nail technician is a profession in its own right and is becoming more more popular all the time. For the right person, it is rewarding, challenging and lucrative. The right person is the one that takes the profession seriously and embarks on a lifetime of learning.

CHAPTER 1

Starting Out: You and Your Industry

INTRODUCTION

This chapter introduces the world of 'nails'. It is an amazingly fast-growing section of the service industry that includes beauty and hair. What used to be an 'add-on' service for some therapists and hairdressers is now a booming business that has its own identity, with many dedicated salons all over the country. There are even many nail salons that offer beauty or hair treatments as an 'add-on' service to the main business of 'nails'. This chapter provides a brief history of the industry, describes the training available and the possible career routes for the nail technician.

ARTIFICIAL NAILS: A BRIEF HISTORY

The art of lengthening nails has been around for centuries, and in many cultures long nails are a symbol of wealth. The ancient Egyptians had shapes made from gold, bone or ivory that could be attached to the end of the finger to indicate wealth and class. Far Eastern cultures have, over the centuries, displayed their social standing by growing their own nails to extreme lengths. The ability to grow nails or wear extended decorations on fingers is meant to show that the person does not do any manual work and has servants or slaves to attend to all their needs.

There are lots of people who have been doing 'nails' for 25–30 years who claim to have been the first to offer artificial nail services in the UK and Europe. They are probably all correct if their concept of the UK and Europe is scaled down to mean their own particular area. Artificial nails as a practice appeared nearly simultaneously in many places, but it was the US that really made a big business of it before any other country. Almost without exception, the idea of creating artificial nails came from the dental industry as inventive people started playing around with the **polymers** and **adhesives** that dental technicians used to create crowns, moulds and other dental appliances. These materials, when mixed, could be formed into a strong solid structure that could go into the mouth, and could also be moulded onto a nail to lengthen or protect it! Small quantities could be applied with a brush and shaped to look like a natural nail. Pigments were already being added to match colours of teeth and a method of etching tooth enamel to allow the material to bond could be modified to work with nails.

The earliest experiments and resultant artificial nails used a **monomer** and polymer mix applied to the nail and extended over a supporting form. This structure hardened and, when the support was removed, was then shaped to look like a natural extension of the nail plate. These dental materials were chemicals that came under the 'family' name of **acrylics**: the acrylic artificial nail was created. All subsequent materials used also belong to the acrylic family but the term 'acrylic nails' has stuck to the method using a **liquid** monomer and **powder** polymer.

Plastic nail shapes that could be stuck onto natural nails with an adhesive had been around for quite a while so it was not long before the shape of these was adapted to create the support for the acrylic structure. Lots of other tools and equipment were used or created to assist this skill. Even dental drills found their way into the equation, as the early acrylics could be so hard that help was needed to shape the nails. An industry grew up to provide the nail technicians (as opposed to dental technicians) with a whole range of accessories.

THE MODERN NAIL TECHNICIAN

Education and skills training

The US did this very well and the public loved the resulting long, painted nails. Eventually colleges included teaching the skill in their cosmetology courses and each of the States included it in their licensing legislation as it became essential to regulate the practice. This is the situation that remains in the US today; students in cosmetology learn the art of artificial nails and, if they want to be a commercial practitioner, they have to achieve their State licence. Each State has different requirements but, essentially, training is usually carried out in a college environment and a set number of hours learning and practising must be completed, followed by a practical exam. Once they have passed this, the individual receives their licence and this allows them to work and purchase products.

The nail companies obviously want to sell their products and many of them provide a 'post-graduate' training service to provide qualified technicians with advanced skills and an understanding of their product range. Of course this does not apply to all companies, as many find selling to the wholesale outlets and mail order via trade magazines sufficient.

The education programme offered by some nail companies can be likened to the skin care companies that provide application techniques and product knowledge to the qualified beauty therapists who will be using their ranges. It can be an important aspect of the product range as correct usage is essential for optimum results and there are usually some techniques that have been developed to make a specific product range different from that of a competitor.

It was this type of post-graduate training, typically of one or two days' duration, that was imported from the US to the UK along with the products. It was training that was designed for qualified technicians who had already learned the basic skills. These short courses were offered in the UK to anyone who was interested in buying products and hundreds of 'technicians' were created who had no theoretical knowledge of the nail and skin, hygiene requirements, legislation or any of the basic information provided in a full qualifying course.

For many years this has been the accepted practice; it has always been assumed that 'nails' is an additional service that can be learned in under a week and has a good profit margin. Fortunately for the future of the industry, it has been becoming more apparent that there is more to it than that. A therapist or hairdresser can learn how to apply nails but not in the same way as learning a new massage technique or a new hair colour range. It is more like adding aromatherapy to a therapist's services or a stylist learning how to perm. Many clients will only ever go to a specialist and many are happy to have one person provide all treatments. There will always be plenty of room for both types of technicians.

As the industry grows, so does the number of nail salons. It is becoming an industry in its own right, recognized by employers, insurers and local authorities. 'Nails' has its own magazines and trade shows, and it now has its own qualifications.

The industry is an exciting place to work in as it is still so new. It is developing and growing, and opportunities for those working within it are becoming wider. 'Nails' is a creative and practical skill and, as such, needs education, practice and dedication. It cannot be learned in a day or two. There are some 'natural' technicians who have good co-ordination and an 'eye' for form, shape, balance and symmetry. Others need to learn how to use the tools and materials and develop their 'eye'. Good training and education is the first step; dedication to practice is the second; the acceptance that no one ever stops learning and improving is the final step to a whole new career and skill.

Career routes

Doing 'nails' is not just about sitting behind a desk and buffing for 8 hours a day. A qualified and experienced technician has a whole world of choices open. The best starting point to be able to choose the routes is to put in the time at that desk. It is a public service and the experience of working with the public is invaluable. Eight career routes are common today: mobile technicians, working from home, being self-employed or employed in a salon, running a salon of your own, teaching or demonstration work or being a media technician. We shall briefly look at all of these.

Mobile technicians

Like hairdressing and most beauty treatments, 'nails' can be a service that can be carried out in a client's home as equipment can be carried. It is a popular choice of a newly trained technician as start-up costs are low. There are many technicians who have made a successful career with a good income.

Requirements: A qualification that is suitable for insurance purposes and local authority licensing if required, such as the **NVQ** Unit in Beauty Therapy Level 3. Experience is not essential as this may be the place a newly qualified technician can gain practice.

Plus points:

- Low start-up costs (no property deposits/mortgages, legal costs, decoration, salon equipment)
- Low overheads (no rent, council taxes, utility bills)
- Flexible working time (no set opening times).

Minus points:

- Lots of travelling time that is not paid for
- Client expectation of lower charges
- Lots of kit carrying
- Less than ideal working situation (working on a dining room or kitchen table).

Things to consider:

- The cost of a car, petrol and car insurance when used for business
- Maintaining good working standards without the stimulus of salon colleagues
- Working in unfavourable conditions that could cause back strain
- Problems of promotion of services, advertising
- Perception: however good the service, the perception of a mobile service has a lower professional status. There are many mobile technicians who do not bother with basic requirements like insurance, and over time this has led to a public view that 'mobile' can mean 'amateur'.

Anyone thinking of starting working in this way should approach it as a business and seek advice from those who understand financial matters. A bank manager can often recommend or be aware of schemes to help a business start up. The Citizens Advice Bureau (CAB) often has information that is useful and the Inland Revenue has many leaflets for self-employed people.

Working from home

A salon can be set up in a private home instead of commercial premises.

Requirements: A qualification that is suitable for insurance purposes and local authority licensing if required, such as the NVQ Unit mentioned above. Experience is not essential as this may be the place a newly qualified technician can gain practice.

Plus points:

- Low overheads
- No travelling
- Can be good for a working parent
- Flexible hours
- Salon atmosphere can be achieved.

Minus points:

- Strangers brought into home
- Lack of stimulus from salon colleagues
- Can disrupt family life.

Things to consider:

- Local authority permission needs to be gained to run a business from a residential property
- Good working practices and hygiene need to be adhered to as odours from products and dust can affect the whole house
- Is access to the salon going to affect the family and security of the home?
- As with a mobile technician, this should be set up as a proper business.

Self-employed in a salon

Clients of most salons, whether hair or beauty, will often ask if the salon 'does nails'. A technician working in a salon on a self-employed basis can be a good relationship. A nail desk takes up so little space that it can usually be squeezed into most salons.

Requirements: As for a mobile technician, but a salon may require experience. It is worth getting personal public and product liability insurance, which is inexpensive via the International Nail Association. The salon may have appropriate insurance, but it may not cover a person who is not employed there and it is not always easy to get a sight of the policy to make sure it is relevant for you.

Plus points:

- Existing potential clients in a commercial environment
- Potential for good promotion with salon staff wearing nails
- Professional atmosphere (hopefully!)
- Less lonely than working alone
- Possibility of sharing promotions and advertising.

Minus points:

- Salon owner may be too demanding
- Staff may not like 'nails' and be unhelpful in recommendations.

Things to consider:

- Care must be taken in the financial arrangement with the salon owner. Being self-employed is a common arrangement but has implications for VAT (if appropriate) and your position with the Inland Revenue. It is usually difficult to get definite answers to questions on tax but the problem usually lies with the salon owner rather than the technician. The technician must ensure that all legal rules are followed for a self-employed person – that is to say, payment of income tax and National Insurance and the keeping of accurate accounts.
- There are several financial arrangements that salon owners can use for this 'rent a space' idea. A weekly or monthly fixed rent is one; the rent can often be high for a technician just starting out but, when the technician becomes busy, it may be low for the salon owner who can see the good income. Under this arrangement, it is best to keep payments from clients separate in order that both parties have an accurate record of client payments.
- Another possibility is to share the payments as a rent, for example 40 per cent to the salon and 60 per cent to the technician. This can help the technician in the early days as there is no rent to pay if there are no clients but a lot of 'rent' will be paid when busy. It can, however, cause tax problems for the owner. There is sometimes the added complication where a salon owner provides the products. In this instance the percentage of payments as 'rent' are usually reversed.
- As with the mobile or home-based technician, this is a business, and should be set up properly.

Employed in a salon

Many employers now require qualified technicians who can provide specialist services for their clients. Many therapists and hairdressers can do 'nails' but they are often too busy or do not like doing it. Also, as it is a practical skill, it needs to be used frequently and with enjoyment to result in good work. It can often make sense for a busy salon to employ a specialist technician.

Requirements: Qualifications are required and, depending on the salon, experience may be necessary. The employer may ask you to carry out a trade test where you can demonstrate your skills. This can be a bit nerve-wracking but just imagine you are dealing with a new client. Again, it is worth having personal insurance, as a client can sue the technician and the salon and it is worth the peace of mind to have the correct cover.

Plus points:

- Guaranteed income
- The salon handles all promotions
- No worries about products, stock and equipment
- Colleagues to work with.

Minus point:

- No independence.

Things to consider:

- Many salons in the service industries pay a basic salary and then commission on treatments and sales on top. In this way, therapists and technicians are encouraged to work well and keep their clients.
- If the 'nails' service is new to the salon, the onus would be on the technician to make it work. As long as the salon is prepared to promote the treatments the technician should produce good work and keep their clients happy and rebooking.

Opening a salon

There are nail salons opening all over the country now and many of them are very successful. Clients often prefer to go to a specialist for a specific service and 'nails' is no exception.

Requirements: Some salon owners have no experience of the services offered and rely on their staff. For working owners it is advisable to have experience of working in a commercial environment together with practical experience. The owner often needs to deal with difficult clients and no amount of training in a school or college will take the place of experience. It is also advisable to have some knowledge of the legal requirements for salons – PAYE, National Insurance, the responsibilities of employers, book keeping, retailing and promotion, health and safety of the premises.

Plus points:

- Total control
- Satisfaction of owning your own business.

Minus points:

- Large financial investment
- Potential problems with staffing
- Permanent commitment
- The need to work long hours or stand in for staff to cover sickness and holidays.

Things to consider:

- As with any new business, there is a great deal of work to do before the doors to the salon open. This work, such as researching the area, creating a viable business plan, making any necessary applications to the local authority, decorating the salon, printing promotional material, recruiting staff and so on, must be done thoroughly and time taken in getting it right. So many businesses fail because the ground work was not properly done.
- Your own business is an exciting prospect and will have a better chance of succeeding if you have spent some time working in a good salon. This experience is invaluable and ensures that lots of mistakes can be avoided.

Teaching

The way in which the industry has grown up has produced a lot of 'nail' trainers, both good and bad. It has been traditional for product companies to have trainers in various parts of the country and this has usually been on a self-employed basis and often connected with the sales of the products. Many training schools have opened (and many have closed) on the strength of income received from short courses and product sales. Private schools and colleges of further education who offer qualifications in beauty therapy often have the facility to teach the 'nail' qualifications and many bring in technicians to teach the subject rather than relying on their beauty therapy lecturers. Usually, a minimum of 3 years' industry experience is required.

Plus points:

- Can be carried out part-time and be additional income and interest
- A very good way of keeping up high standards
- Job satisfaction (and often frustration) in teaching new skills to students
- If connected to a product company, there is involvement with the industry as a whole.

Minus points:

- Full-time teaching of 'nails' is hard to find
- If self-employed and connected to a company, there is no guaranteed income.

Things to consider:

- A good technician does not necessarily make a good teacher, and vice versa.
- To become a good teacher it is worth learning teaching skills in addition to 'nail' skills. If working in a college, it is usually necessary to be a qualified Vocational Assessor.
- Part-time teaching can often fit very well with working in a salon. You will be bringing real experience to your students, supplementing your income and gaining variety in your working life.

Sales/demonstrator

Product companies often have a sales person who visits salons to sell and demonstrate products and technicians who demonstrate on stands at trade shows.

Requirements: A skilled technician would suit this job and one who had understanding of how products worked. Experience in sales would also be a bonus. Personality is very important as it needs an outgoing person who communicates well with people. Qualifications are always desirable and personal insurance is recommended. It is unlikely that a set period of experience would be required, but is obviously preferable.

Plus points:

- Variety of work
- Involvement in the wider industry
- Usually part-time, so could fit around clients.

Minus points:

- Full-time jobs are rare
- Part-time jobs may be casual (that is, only when required).

Things to consider:

There are not many companies that are large enough to employ full-time sales reps. Many have part-time technicians who are either employed or self-employed and work on a commission basis. Demonstrators are often technicians connected with the company who are prepared to work at trade shows.

Media technicians

The nail industry is beginning to achieve a higher profile in the market and people are becoming more aware of 'nails' as being part of grooming and fashion. A separate person to do 'nails' on photographic shoots and catwalk shows is now acceptable (if the budget allows).

Requirements: A high level of skill, creativity and imagination. Insurance is essential. Patience and discretion are essential commodities. The level of skill is more important than time spent working but this technician will often be called upon to solve many different problems and nothing takes the place of experience.

Plus points:

- Wide variety of work
- Chance of meeting and working with famous people
- High fees for some types of work
- High profile for technician.

Minus points:

- Work not regular
- Long hours of waiting around following frantic working sessions
- Dealing with sometimes difficult people
- Carrying a very heavy kit
- Working very long hours on some jobs
- Lots of free or low-paid work in order to achieve the recognition for paid work.

Things to consider:

At the present time there are very few technicians who get 'published' in the media. Lots appear in trade magazines. Media work is a very different world and technicians need to be like make-up artists and hairdressers who can help create images for advertising, editorial work and fashion shows. A portfolio of work needs to be compiled to show prospective employers. As a general 'rule of thumb', work that receives credits (that is, the person's name with the pictures) is usually low-paid or even free; work that does not receive credits is usually paid for by way of a fee. It is advisable to use the services of an agent as most magazines, advertising agencies, designers and photographers are used to using an agent to arrange for the creative team to attend. Agents obviously charge a fee but the potential earnings of this kind of work are very high.

This list of career routes is not exhaustive, there are many variants and combinations. The industry is an exciting place to be and there is a place for everyone. Artificial nails is not the only skill and treatment involved; there are many who specialize in natural nail care, and it seems that the majority of European women prefer natural nails to artificial even if they have used the artificial variety to help them on their way.

The most important message is that recognized qualifications, practise, dedication and a lifetime of learning is essential for real success.

SUMMARY

This chapter has sketched the education and skills training required by the modern nail technician and outlined the eight most common career paths the technician can follow, highlighting the advantages and disadvantages of each. The legislative/health and safety requirements of self- or salon employment are also made clear, and the potential hazards for both client and technician of their non-observance.

CHAPTER 2

Anatomy and Physiology of Skin and the Nail Unit

INTRODUCTION

This chapter provides all the essential theoretical information about the skin and nails, the parts of the body that are affected by the application of artificial nails. It covers all the requirements of the National Occupational Standards and puts the treatment in the context of the potential problems of an individual client.

ESSENTIAL KNOWLEDGE

Hairdressers learn about the structure of hair, how it grows and where it comes from; beauty therapists learn about the structure of skin, the underlying muscles and bones and the basic working of the human body. They do this in order to understand the area that is being treated, how to vary treatments for individuals, how to recognize potential problems and how to put right what may go wrong. Nail technicians must do the same. They must learn about the area of the human body they are dealing with. This will ensure that they work safely, understand when and how to adapt treatments, give the best possible advice to their clients and know how to deal with problems.

A **natural nail** is an adaptation of the skin and is surrounded by skin. By understanding how the skin is formed and why helps to understand how a nail is created and what may be happening if the nail is growing less than perfectly. A thorough knowledge of this part of the body is the basis of essential knowledge because it will:

- Help you to *recognize any disorders* and understand what may have caused them
- Demonstrate a knowledge and understanding of the area being worked on during treatments, by the ability to answer any question the client may ask; this will *promote professionalism and generate confidence*

- Help you to choose the *most suitable products for the client* and understand their effects on the skin and nails.

THE SKIN

The skin is the largest organ of the human body and plays many essential roles. It is protective, helps with temperature control and is involved in one of the senses: touch.

The skin over the whole of the body has basically the same structure but has some local variations, e.g. thickness, blood and nerve supply, colour, etc. Hair and nails are made of modified skin cells.

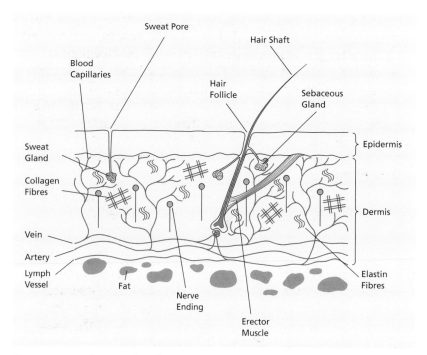

Cross-section through the skin

Functions

Skin has eight main functions for the body.

1. Protection

Skin provides a waterproof coat that protects the body from dirt, minor injuries, bacterial infection and chemical attack.

- The first barrier is a mixture of oil (**sebum**) and **sweat** which forms a slightly acidic film over its surface. This discourages the growth of **bacteria** and **fungus**. The sebum, the natural oil produced by sebaceous glands in the hair **follicles** of the skin, creates a waterproof coating which helps prevent the skin lose essential water and, to a certain extent, also prevents the skin from absorbing too much water externally. This effect is minimal as the skin can be quite absorbent, especially when it suffers from dryness.

- The second barrier is the uppermost layer of the skin (**stratum corneum**) which can act as a filter against invading bacteria. The healthy construction of this barrier provides good protection but it is very easily damaged. It relies on a good level of natural moisture to hold the **keratinized** skin cells together. On the hands, especially, this moisture is very often lost owing to environmental damage (detergents, water and so on).
- The third barrier is the production of a pigment called **melanin** in the skin, which protects lower tissues against **ultraviolet (UV) light** damage.
- Although not a barrier, the skin does have an early warning system of invasion of a chemical that the body will not tolerate or is sensitive or allergic to. Irritation on any part of the skin is usually a sign that an **allergic reaction** is starting. If the **allergen** (substance that is causing the reaction) is promptly removed the reaction should subside. This is more common when a reaction to a substance is applied deliberately or otherwise to the skin but can be a result of a substance from inside the body that has been ingested (via the mouth) or inhaled (by breathing in).

2. Sensation

There are several different nerve endings carried in the skin which respond to heat, cold, touch, pressure and pain.

3. Heat regulation

The skin helps to keep the body at a constant temperature of 37°C. It is able to do this in several ways: dilation or constriction of the blood vessels (**capillaries**) near the surface of the skin contain heat or allow it to escape; sweat, produced by the sweat glands, evaporates and cools the body; and fat in the **subcutaneous layer** insulates the body.

4. Excretion

Perspiration and some waste products, such as water and salt are lost through the skin.

5. Secretion

Sebum, which moisturizes and protects, is produced in the sebaceous glands.

6. Vitamin D formation

The skin is able to produce **Vitamin D** through the action of ultraviolet light. This vitamin is essential to the absorption of calcium.

7. Storage

The skin stores fat and water that can be used by any part of the body as necessary.

8. Absorption

Some substances can be absorbed through the skin and will stay in the area or go into the blood stream and be carried throughout the body. (The effect of overabsorption can be seen after a good soak in the bath!) This absorbency can be useful when applying nourishing products to it but can also be quite the reverse; the skin can allow penetration of harmful substances. Absorption through the skin is one of the routes of entry of the human body for chemicals together with **inhalation** and **ingestion**. The skin should be protected when using potentially harmful substances and chances of absorption should be minimized.

Classes of skin

There are two main classes of skin; both types are found on the hands and feet.

Thick hairless skin

This is found on the palms of the hands and the soles of the feet. As the name suggests, this type does not have any hair follicles and therefore has no oil-producing glands which makes it prone to dryness. It has many sweat glands, which assist in gripping objects, and heightens sensitivity. Certain layers of the skin in this type are thicker and ridged to allow for wear and tear and to give a 'non-slip' surface.

Thin, hairy skin

This covers much of the body and along with the many structures found in all skin, has hair follicles.

Layers of skin

It can be seen from the earlier diagram that there are three main layers of skin: the **epidermis**, the **dermis** and the subcutaneous layer. In carrying out hand, feet and nail treatments, we are more concerned with the structure of the epidermis although the dermis does play some part.

The epidermis

Cells in the epidermis: The epidermis is of special interest as nails are evolutionary adaptations of this cell-producing area, as are hair, hooves, horns, scales and feathers. It is this layer that is treated in manicures and pedicures and an improvement to the condition of this layer is what is most required by clients requiring a manicure.

The epidermis consists of layers of skin cells in various stages of development, growth, adaptation and death. The adaptation will depend on where in the body the skin is situated:

- In a hair follicle the cells will form a hair
- In the **matrix** of the nail, they will form a **nail plate**

- In areas exposed to ultraviolet light, they will produce more melanin
- On the palms of hands and soles of feet, the clear layer **(stratum lucidum)** will be much thicker.

This progression of cells takes place from the lower level of the epidermis up through to the surface of the skin. The cells go through many changes during this journey. The progression of a skin cell in an area of skin that does not require any adaptations and is normal and healthy takes around 4–6 weeks. Skin disorders or other general health problems can influence this process. The little skin cell ends up keratinized, flat and non-living and part of the protective stratum corneum. It is eventually shed from the skin and often found in house dust (or the inside of a pair of tights!).

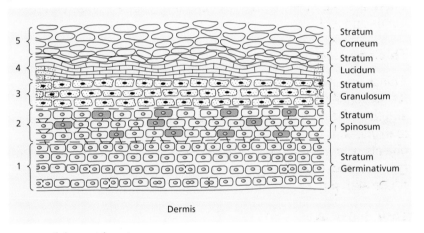

Layers of the epidermis

Layers in the epidermis:

1 The base layer or **stratum germinativum** is where the skin cells are formed and is responsible for the growth of the epidermis. They contain melanin and the early stages of **keratin**, which is a protein, and will eventually form either a protective layer on the top of the skin or be adapted to form nails or hair.

   The cells here are continually dividing and reproducing themselves. This is a process called **mitosis**. The cells are plump, surrounded by the porous cell membrane, full of cellular fluid called **cytoplasm** and with an active nucleus that is responsible for cell reproduction and function and carries the genes inherited from our parents.

   As these cells divide and reproduce themselves they are pushed up and into the next layer of the epidermis.

2 The **stratum spinosum**, or prickle-cell layer, is where most of the cells have developed spines that connect them to surrounding cells. The nucleus is becoming less active as reproduction has slowed down or stopped.

   Some of the cells have adapted into **melanocytes** that produce the pigment melanin. These are the cells that help protect the lower layers of the skin from ultraviolet damage from the sun. The amount of melanocytes depends on our skin colour. Black skins that have evolved from very hot countries, for example, have significantly more melanin for maximum protection. Fairer-skinned people that tend to come from the colder countries have much less pigment. Fair-skinned people that have been sunbathing or using a sunbed have developed extra melanocytes for their protection and this is what appears as a suntan. Sunburn is where too much radiation from the sun has been on the skin before melanocytes have been formed to protect it. This radiation has been able to penetrate to lower levels and could cause problems in later life. There is a great deal of advice becoming available now as the effects of overexposure to the sun's radiation are understood.

The amount of melanin can vary in the same area of skin. Patches of darker skin can be evident, sometimes on the back of the hands, face or chest. This is an overproduction of melanin and is stimulated by ultraviolet radiation, but is more usually caused by a hormone inbalance, for example during pregnancy or when taking a contraceptive pill. In older people, 'liver spots' on the back of the hand are caused by minor **sun damage** throughout their life. Freckles are also the result of sun damage and often found on lighter skins that are more prone to suffering from overexposure.

There is an opposite effect to the overproduction of melanin which results in lighter patches on the skin. This is called **vitiligo** or **leucoderma**, and it is where the skin has lost its ability to produce melanin. There is also a condition where the whole of the skin is unable to produce melanin, called **albinism**. These people have very light skin and their hair and eyes lack colour.

None of these conditions is infectious but skin often needs extra protection and the hands are the areas of the body which often suffer the most.

3 The **stratum granulosum**, or granular layer, is where the cells are beginning to die. They appear much less plump and the nucleus is beginning to break up. The cytoplasm (or cellular fluid) is thickening and becoming granular where the protein keratin is beginning to form.

4 The stratum lucidum, or clear layer, is an adapted layer that is found only in the palms of the hand and soles of the feet – that is, the thick hairless class of skin. This extra layer gives specific characteristics to these areas. The hands and feet need to grip: the hands to hold things and the feet to grip the ground. This clear layer helps to form the dips and ridges in our hands and feet that are known as our 'finger or hand prints' (our feet also have the same 'prints'). The skin in these areas does not produce sebum (natural oil) as it does not have any hair follicles: oil would make our hands and feet slippery. This area of skin only produces sweat from millions of sweat glands. A small amount of sweat together with the ridges and

TIP

Women, in particular, sometimes find darker patches on the sides of their neck. This is often due to the reaction of the sun on an area of skin that has had perfume sprayed on.

dips help our grip. Too much sweat also makes our skin slippery and is usually a hormonal effect arising from an emotional moment such as fright or nervousness. Some people produce an excess amount of sweat on the palms of their hands. If 'slippery' hands are noticed, then the technician should take extra care in preparing the nail (see Chapter 5).

5   The stratum corneum, or cornified layer, is the uppermost layer of skin. The cells have flattened, lost their nucleus and all the cytoplasm and become keratinized. The flat cells are held together in a type of 'brick-wall' arrangement by intercellular cement mostly composed of lipids, a natural fat produced by the skin together with sebum and sweat and keratin bonds. This forms a wonderful barrier and protection for the skin but is easily damaged, especially on the hands.

As newly keratinized cells are pushed up, the older flakes of dead skin are shed in a process called **desquamation** where the bonds are broken down. This will happen naturally but often happens quicker as the intercellular cement is broken down by environmental excesses such as pollution or hard water.

There are many conditions that affect this whole cycle and there are skin disorders that can speed up the process, such as psoriasis, or slow it down.

It is really important for a nail technician to understand this process as not only must the skin surrounding the nail and that on the hand be cared for, but it is also the basis of how nails are formed.

Below the epidermis is another part of the skin that is very different and much thicker, called the dermis.

The dermis

This layer carries the many structures within the skin such as nerves, blood capillaries, nerve endings, sweat ducts that open onto the surface of the skin as pores, sebaceous glands that open into hair follicles. It helps to serve the epidermis by carrying a vast network of capillaries and gives it structural support.

Fibres in the dermis: One of the main features of the dermis is the network of strong fibres of which there are two types: **collagen** and **elastin**. They are both made of protein.

Collagen acts as a support to the skin and keeps it firm and gives it a plump, youthful appearance. Elastin gives the skin its elastic properties, allowing it to move and stretch but then return to its original position. In young skin, both types of fibres are plentiful but as the skin ages the fibres start to break down and are not replaced so readily. The lack of collagen allows the skin to form into wrinkles between muscles and lack of elastin allows the skin to become softer and less firm.

The skin on the back of the hands does not always demonstrate a person's exact biological age as it is prone to misuse and damage. The skin of the face is usually more cared for and can often appear younger than the person's actual age. Conversely, hands often give away age and can look older than necessary. The skin on the backs of the hands has very little support in the way of muscles and stored fat. It does however have some very strong tendons that move the fingers and large blood vessels that supply the hand. As the elastin and collagen become less effective owing to age and damage from ultraviolet light and weather, the tendons and blood vessels become more apparent and thus giving an ageing appearance.

Other structures in the dermis:

- **Nerves**. The dermis carries a vast network of nerve endings that send a whole host of messages back to the brain where the messages are 'decoded' and any work that the body needs to do is sent to the relevant areas. The nerves give us our sense of touch and our finger tips are some of the most sensitive areas of our body. In addition to the ability to feel, the nerves are also a form of protection. If extreme heat is touched, the nerves send an emergency message to the brain; the brain recognizes the emergency and sends another message, via the nervous system, to the muscles which move the relevant area of the body away from the danger. All this happens in a fraction of a second.
- **Blood vessels**. These are a network of fine capillaries carrying blood to maintain the health of the skin. Blood carries nutrients (food) and oxygen to every cell in the body and removes waste products. The blood plays several essential roles in the working of the whole body. With regard to the skin, the main roles are connected with heat regulation. If the body is becoming too hot, the blood vessels dilate (become bigger) within the skin. This assists heat loss. The reverse happens if the body is becoming too cold: the vessels constrict, keeping the blood deeper within the body to conserve heat.

    If the skin is damaged by a superficial cut, the tiny capillaries are severed and the skin bleeds. Some of the cells that form blood are capable of forming together and creating a clot that blocks the ruptured vessels and prevents more blood loss. The redness seen around a cut or other damage is an increase in the blood supply as it helps the cells to repair themselves.

    Increased blood supply in the skin causing a redness without obvious damage could be the body's defence system in action. A harmful body (such a splinter) or substance could have entered the skin and is causing an irritation. Cells within the dermis called mast cells release a chemical called **histamine** that increases the blood supply to the area; this action attempts to destroy the invader. This defence mechanism can progress from a slight redness, to itching and progress to blisters and swelling. If the allergen (the

TIP

A gentle pinch to the skin on the back of the hand demonstrates age and condition. A young and hydrated skin recovers immediately. Older and/or dehydrated skin takes longer to recover. Experiment on different skin to discover the difference.

TIP

If a client has suffered a serious illness or sustained damage to their hand or fingers, they may have lost sensation to some areas. Make sure this is not the case by asking tactful questions or gently pressing areas with a cuticle knife. A client with limited or lack of sensation can be easily damaged!

TIP

If an area of skin feels warm to the touch (for example, the side wall of a nail) and appears red, there is an infection present and work on nails should be avoided completely.

substance that is causing an allergic reaction) or irritant is removed at the first hint of trouble, the reactions will often subside. If not, the condition can continue and result in a distressing and painful type of **dermatitis**.

- **Lymph vessels**: Like the network of blood vessels, another system carries a fluid called lymph around the body. **Lymph** is similar in many ways to blood in that it circulates to all the cells and carries a certain amount of nutrients, but its main role is as our body's defence mechanism. The lymph fights and removes bacteria and other invasions and removes excess fluid from cells and surrounding tissue. The lymphatic fluid is 'filtered' by lymph glands sited all over the body. When the body is fighting an infection of some description glands, often in the neck, can feel swollen and tender.

  The lymphatic system does not have a pump to move it around in the way that the blood has the heart. It relies, instead, on muscular movement to push it along. The flow of lymph can sometimes be sluggish and excess fluid and waste can build up in certain areas.

  There are no lymph glands sited near the feet and gravity will often cause excess fluid to collect in this area. Glands are at the top of the leg in the groin. The nearest glands to the hands are on the inside of the elbows. Massage in these areas with movements towards the glands can help to increase circulation and reduce excess fluid.

- **Sweat glands**: Sweat glands, with their own blood supply, are sited in the dermis and a tube, or duct, leads directly from the gland through the dermis and epidermis to open onto the surface and is seen as a pore in the skin. There are more sweat glands on the palms of the hands and soles of the feet than anywhere else on the body.

  The most common type of gland, **eccrine glands**, are found all over the body and help to regulate the body's heat by secreting small amounts of sweat all the time. Another, less common type, are **apocrine glands**, that are sited under the arm and groin. The sweat secreted from these has a different chemical composition and the sweat production is controlled by hormones.

- **Hair follicles**: Another structure found in the dermis of the skin are hair follicles (with the exception of the palms of the hands, the soles of the feet and the lips). A follicle is a long sack-like shape where epidermal tissue extends from the surface of the skin down through the epidermis and dermis to its own blood supply. At the base of the follicle is an area called the germinal matrix where certain epidermal cells are 'instructed' by their nucleus to adapt their growth and form together to create a hair. As in the epidermis, the new cells push the older ones upward and the hair grows up the follicle and out through the surface of the skin.

- **Sebaceous glands**: Connected to the follicle is another structure: the sebaceous gland. This secretes the natural oil,

TIP

Some people produce more sweat on their hands. This can be an indication of excessive moisture in the nail plate. It is worth taking extra care in the dehydration stage of nail preparation and repeating the process several times.

sebum, onto the hair shaft and the skin's surface. The oil helps to lubricate the hair shaft and plays an important role in the skin's protective functions. It helps create the waterproof barrier and therefore keep moisture in the cells of the skin and it also, together with sweat, creates a slightly acidic covering on the skin that acts as a bactericide and discourages growth of unwanted micro-organisms. This covering is known as the **acid mantle**.

- **pH values**: For the skin to remain healthy it needs to maintain the degree of acidity created by the sebum and sweat. If this changes too much the skin can become dry and if it changes drastically the skin is damaged. Acidity and alkalinity is measured by a scale called the **pH value**. Low numbers (1–7) are acidic and high numbers (7–14) are alkaline. A value of 7 is neutral. Examples of **acids** can be found in citric fruits, such as lemons. This level of acidity would not damage the skin unless it was left on it for a period of time. Fruit acids are usually the base of a popular ingredient in skin care: **AHA** (alpha hydroxy acids). These can be useful in skin care as they can help remove dead skin cells and debris from the surface of the skin and help generate cell renewal in areas that need assistance, such as the face and backs of the hands. Acids with low pH values would 'burn' the skin, causing extreme irritation and blisters.

  At the other end of the scale are the **alkalines** that can have a similar effect on the skin. The milder alkalines are often used in skin treatments. Sodium hydroxide is sometimes used to soften and remove unwanted skin cells, for example in a cuticle remover. Soap is alkaline and is very drying to the skin. Extreme alkalines, such as household bleach, will damage skin in the same way that acids will.

  The pH value of the skin is naturally 5.5–5.6 – that is, slightly acidic, and skin preparations that are often called 'pH balanced' will have a similar pH value.

  Another structure attached to the hair folicle is a tiny muscle, the arrector pili muscle. This contracts and causes the hair to stand upright in the skin. It does this to help trap heat and also as a response to some emotional reactions. The effect is usually known as 'goose bumps'.

Below the level of the dermis is a layer of stored fat. This fat is a supply of energy for the body and also helps contain heat within the body.

THE NAIL UNIT

A basic understanding of how the skin is structured and how it grows should help with understanding how finger and toe nails are formed as a **nail unit**. Like the hair follicle, the area where the nail starts life is a fold of the epidermal layer where skin cells are instructed by their nucleus to make certain adaptations. In the skin they become keratinized to form the flattened cells of the stratum corneum. In a hair, they are keratinized and adapted to create a hair shaft. In a nail, they are also keratinized and form flat layers that make up a hard nail plate. Like the upper layer of the epidermis (stratum corneum) and hair, the nail is non-living. Like hair it can be cut without any sensation.

The function of the nail

All species of primate have nails. They are linked to the evolution of using hands (and feet) to manipulate objects. Humans, however, are the only animal able to use the thumb and forefinger in a pincer movement. The higher primates, such as gorillas and chimpanzees, have hands that are very similar to ours with fingerprints and perfect nails, but they cannot manipulate their thumbs as we can. There is even a theory that this arrangement of our thumbs gave our species the opportunity to evolve faster as we were able to use a wider variety of tools.

Nails are on the end of our fingers for several reasons and are not just there to paint or chew! They provide a rigid support for the end of the finger, allowing us to pick things up easier, and they protect the end of the finger and the last bone from countless knocks.

Nails start to form in an unborn baby very early in the gestation period and by 17–20 weeks are fully formed. Nails will even grow for a short period after death as the cycle of adaptation of the skin cells and keratinization will continue, once it has started, without any nourishment from the blood supply.

The structure of the nail

Matrix

This is the most important area of the nail unit. It is directly under the **proximal nail fold** or **mantle** and it is where the skin cells are adapted to form the nail plate. As the skin cells become keratinized they bond together and lose the other cell contents. Unlike in the epidermis where the bonds break down and the cells are shed, the bonds in newly forming nail plate are much stronger and the **lipid** content is retained. The keratinized cells form layers, or lamellar, and several of these bond together to form the nail plate.

The shape and size of the matrix will determine the thickness and width of the nail. The matrix extends from the base of the nail down towards the first joint. The longer the matrix, the thicker the nail. Thin nails will tend to have a short matrix. The width of the nail will be determined by the width of the matrix. Therefore it follows that naturally thin (or thick) nails are hereditary; however, a lot can happen to them once they are grown to change this characteristic.

The developing nail in the matrix is very soft until full keratinization has taken place and damage to this area can result in a permanently deformed nail. An example of this could be a person who has shut their finger in a door, even as a child. If the

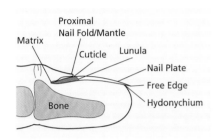

Cross-section of the nail unit

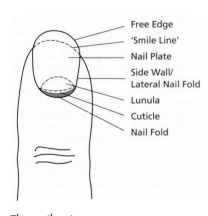

The nail unit

area of the matrix is damaged, the base of the nail and the nail plate may have a permanent ridge. Another example would be if someone had a serious infection in the area. If damage to the area is temporary and heals properly in the matrix, any deformity to the nail should grow out in approximately 6 months after the damage has healed.

Proximal nail fold or mantle

The epidermis of the skin of the finger, above the matrix, folds back on itself and underneath. As in the hair follicle, the deeper area of the fold forms part of the germinal matrix and helps protect the area.

This area of skin can often be quite large and unsightly. This can happen when it is stuck to the cuticle, the nail grows and pulls the skin with it. When the skin is overstretched it splits, usually at the sides, and appears ragged. These splits can be quite sore and, if pulled, can become infected and inflamed. The split piece of skin can be very carefully removed with cuticle nippers. Proper care of the nails ensures that the nail fold does not stick to the nail plate as it is regularly lifted away. This area should not be pushed as this can cause damage to the underlying soft nail and matrix. When the nails are soaked in water or softened with oils, the nail fold can be lifted with ease. It is not recommended that the lifted skin is cut on a regular basis. The body is expert at protecting itself and if an area is removed often the body will compensate and grow thicker skin. If the skin has been lifted for the first time and is unsightly, careful removal may be carried out with a hygienic pair of nippers, used correctly. The area should then be treated with oil or cream to keep the skin soft and prevent it from sticking to the cuticle.

Lateral nail fold or side wall

The skin of the finger folds down along the side of the nail and provides the nail plate with protection and a groove to guide the growth of the nail. A seal is formed here to prevent invasion of unwanted substances or micro-organisms.

Eponychium

This is an area at the base of the nail plate where the proximal nail fold meets the nail plate. It acts as a seal for that area of the nail and guards against invasive bacteria. During a manicure, this area should be treated gently as, if the seal is broken, it is not only painful but infection can occur.

The cuticle

The nail fold is often called the cuticle, but this is inaccurate. The underside of the proximal nail fold constantly sheds a layer of clear skin that sits on the nail plate and grows with it. This is the real cuticle and is not always visible until softened. This is the

TIP

A way to remember the difference between '**proximal**' and '**distal**' is to think of proximal 'being in the proximity of', that is, 'close to' the body; distal is 'at a distance', that is, 'away' from the body. These names apply to several structures in anatomy and 'close' relates to the centre of the body.

TIP

A way to remember '**lateral**' is to remember 'lateral thinking', which could be described as 'sideways' thinking.

skin that should be removed during a manicure and always before the application of artificial nails to avoid any lifting problems as products do not bond with skin, only with the nail plate. This skin is sometimes called the pterygium. When using a cuticle knife it is usually possible to feel the difference between skin and hard nail even if the skin is not visible. As the epidermis of the nail fold produces this layer continuously, there is always some to be found on the nail plate, however small.

The nail plate

As previously explained, keratinized skin cells form the nail plate. These flattened cells stick together and form layers. There are not as many lipids (fats) in the nails and there are many air spaces; this allows ten times as much water to be absorbed by the nail than by the skin. This can be seen when the nails are soaked in water, e.g. the bath. They become very transparent and flexible. **Evaporation** of water soaked up by the nails can be quite damaging as it breaks down the structures that hold the cells together and cause weak and peeling nails.

The uppermost layer of nail is formed in the deepest part of the matrix, while the lower layers are formed nearer the cuticle. This results in a very hard surface and much softer lower layer of the nail plate.

When nails become too dry and peel, not only are they thinner, but the hard upper layer has been lost leaving the pliable and weaker lower layers. Nails must be protected from this condition which is why wearing of gloves for washing up, etc. is always recommended. Nail varnish can also help protect the nails, as can massaging oils or cream into the cuticle area.

As the nail plate leaves the end of the finger, it forms a projection called the **free edge**. This appears whiter than the main body of the nail as it is not attached to the nail bed.

The nail plate has a proximal and distal area and the free edge could be described as the distal edge.

Lunula

This is also known as the half moon, an area of the nail by or under the proximal nail fold, and the front end of the matrix. It appears whiter because the cells are not yet completely keratinized and not totally transparent. Not every person has an exposed lunula and it is a misconception that the lunula (or half moon) should be visible. The nail is still slightly soft in this area and easily damaged so, if anything, it is better that the lunula is protected by the nail fold. People who have a large exposed lunula usually have very ridged nails which is often more noticeable on the thumbs. This is due to continual trauma to the soft nail from everyday living. During a manicure or any work done in the cuticle area, care must be taken not to press too hard on the lunula as it will cause a ridge in the nail which will need to grow up and off the end before it disappears.

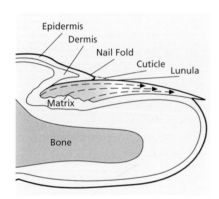

Growth of the nail plate from the matrix

The nail bed

This lies directly under the nail plate. It is skin just like on the rest of the body, but has a very rich supply of blood and lymph vessels to keep the nail healthy. It also has a series of ridges and grooves that fit into ridges and grooves on the underside of the nail plate. These are what hold the nail onto the nail bed. If the ridges are disturbed or if the nail plate becomes too thin and flexible, this 'hold' is broken and causes the nail plate to separate from the nail bed. This is a dangerous situation as it allows bacteria in under the nail that could develop and cause severe problems. Nail technicians must take extreme care not to over-buff the nail as this will cause the nail to become too thin. If this thinning occurs anywhere on the nail, it will eventually grow up to the end of the nail bed where it is most likely to result in separation.

The nail plate appears pink in this area, owing to the colour of the underlying skin.

The hyponychium

This is the area of skin at the very end of the nail bed under the beginning of the free edge. It forms a very tight seal that prevents bacteria, **fungi** and **viruses** from entering. There are many nerve endings in this area which act as a warning to this seal being broken. Sometimes, this area grows under the free edge, especially those with almond shaped nails, and forms an area which can be painful if pushed. It is thought to be a form of support to the free edge and care must be taken not to disturb it. This is sometimes called the **solehorn**.

Like all areas of skin, the epidermis sheds dead skin cells continuously. These cells can often be found under the free edge, especially of the toenails, where they get trapped.

The onychodermal band

This is the area of the hyponychium and a slight change of colour in the skin can be seen. When applying a **French manicure** or artificial nails using a **white-tip powder** or **gel**, it is referred to as the **'smile line'** and its ideal shape should mirror the shape at the base of the nail to create a symmetrical 'top and bottom'.

THE PROCESS OF NAIL GROWTH

Rates of growth

Like hair, nails grow at different rates in individuals and different times of the year. As an average guide, nails grow at the rate of between 0.5–1.2 mm per week and it takes approximately 5–6 months for a nail to grow from the matrix to the free edge. The growth rate is faster in the summer and during pregnancy and usually slows down with age. It can be speeded up or slowed down by illness.

The speed or strength of nail growth is not linked specifically to diet, vitamin or mineral intake but can be improved, along with the condition of skin and hair, if a well-balanced diet is followed. It is quite common to notice the effects of systemic trauma on the nails. For example, a general anaesthetic, bereavement, illness, etc. will often show up as a line or ridge on the nail plate where the growth has been affected.

Technicians and their clients will often notice an increased growth rate immediately after artificial nails have been applied. This is owing to the stimulation produced by buffing during application. The nail matrix and nail bed have a concentrated supply of blood and lymph vessels that supply the area with nutrients and remove waste products. Stimulation of the circulation in this area will improve this function and assist growth.

Buffing the natural nail during a manicure is a valuable treatment but care must be taken not to thin the nail or create too much heat through friction, as this can cause splitting.

The effect of stimulation to the circulation can be seen in the general growth of nails: nails on the dominant hand grow faster, as does the forefinger. Nail biters have faster growing nails owing to the continual nibbling.

As a technician, the growth rate of an individual's nails will affect maintenance treatments (see Chapter 5). Artificial nails must be maintained to compensate for this growth. The majority of clients will need to return every 2–3 weeks, but some clients need to return only every 4–5 weeks, as their growth rate is slower.

Nail composition and strength

Keratin and amino acids

The skin cells that are formed in the matrix have, in their nucleus, the 'instructions' to keratinize but, unlike the keratinized skin cells of the stratum corneum that form a barrier and then are lost, these cells form together to create the hard nail plate layers.

Keratin is a type of **protein** that is made in the body and the body has many different proteins that are essential to the body's function. Proteins are made up of certain sequences of **amino acids**. Amino acids are chemicals created by the body that, when linked together in various but specific sequences, make the various proteins. The linked amino acids form long 'strands' and these strands are linked together at intervals with another amino acid, bonding the strands together and creating a strong structure. The keratin of the nail has many more of these bonds than that of skin and hair.

Hard and soft nails

The progression of cells from the matrix to the nail plate is very similar to those making the journey in the epidermis of the skin.

> **TIP**
>
> An excellent stimulation for nails to encourage faster and healthier growth is to place the hands together, like praying, curling the fingers in so the nails touch each other and rubbing them back and forth to produce a clicking sound.

The cells are created by cell division deep in the matrix and, as they are pushed forward, lose the cellular fluid and become flatter. The lunular is thought to be an area where this process has not quite finished, hence its whiter appearance. As the cells are pushed forward by the reproducing cells behind they become completely keratinized, flat and hard. Therefore the nail plate nearest to the nail fold is softer than the distal edge, and can be easily damaged.

TIP

The upper layer of the nail plate has come from the deepest part of the matrix and is therefore harder as it is older. The lowest layer is the youngest, having come from the distal (furthest away from the hand) part of the matrix and is therefore softer.

- A strong nail is one that can withstand breakage. This does not necessarily mean hard as 'hard' could suggest **brittleness** and the nail could easily snap. Many products on the market are nail 'strengtheners' which can mean nail 'hardeners'. If a weak nail is hardened too much, it will become brittle. If a hard or brittle nail becomes too soft and flexible, it will tear. The spaces between ketatinized cells are full of moisture from the nail bed beneath and from external sources. The right amount of moisture will keep the nail flexible and help absorb shocks. Too much, and the nail bends, too little and the nail becomes dry and brittle.
- The nail plate is very absorbent and too much water can cause splitting and peeling. Excessive water can cause the nail plate to soften and swell. Repeated softening and swelling can cause surface peeling.
- The only truly effective moisturizer for skin and nails is water, but in the right amount. Using creams and oils is beneficial as they can seal natural moisture in and keep too much out. Solvents, such as acetone and nail varnish removers, can remove natural oils and water and can be the cause of dryness if overused.
- The perfect nail is a combination of strength and **flexibility**. A nail specialist should be able to diagnose the exact condition of a client's nails and be able to recommend the ideal treatment and products. It may be that a weak nail may need a hardening treatment for a period of time followed by a moisturizing treatment. A brittle nail may need moisturizing then hardening. Understanding of nail growth and structure brings with it the ability to correctly diagnose conditions.

Protein, calcium and nails

As mentioned before, nails are keratinized skin cells. Keratin is a protein composed of amino acids formed together in long chains and linked by an amino acid bond. The vast number of these strong bonds is specific to nails and is what makes them so much harder than skin and hair. The protein, keratin, is mostly composed of carbon, oxygen, nitrogen, sulphur and hydrogen. The nail plate also has traces of many other chemicals, e.g. iron, zinc, sodium, calcium, titanium, even aluminium, copper, gold and silver.

There are many myths about calcium and nails. The body's intake and absorption of calcium is essential for teeth and bones but as calcium is only 0.07 per cent of the nail, it does not play a large part. The body needs Vitamin D in order to absorb calcium and that is obtained from the sun and diet. If this vitamin is lacking, conditions such as rickets can occur. White spots on the nail are often blamed on a lack of calcium but this is usually incorrect (see Chapter 9). They are usually caused by trauma to the nail plate causing minor separation of the layers. In rare instances, the spots may be caused by lack of the trace element, zinc, in the body but a reasonable diet and good health does not cause this condition.

The artificial nail and the natural nail

The strength of the nail can be influenced even during the wearing of artificial nails or varnish. The nail plate is at its softest in the area of the cuticle and there should be a narrow margin of nail that is not covered. A nourishing oil massaged into this area daily will affect the new nail growing, so weak or brittle nails can be improved while artificial nails are worn. The massaging will stimulate the area and the oil will help to reduce the moisture loss from the new nail. If the artificial nails are correctly maintained, the natural nails should be stronger when they are removed.

Can artificial nails damage natural nails? They certainly can if they are incorrectly applied or the wearer does not understand how to look after them properly. Damage to natural nails is usually caused by an inexperienced or unprofessional technician or an uneducated client. It is really important that technicians explain what the wearer needs to do (or not do) in between treatments.

TIP

Nails that are naturally thick or thin are hereditary. A longer matrix will produce a thick nail. Conversely, a short matrix can produce only a thinner nail.

SUMMARY

This chapter has explained the basic anatomy and physiology of skin and nails, nail structure and growth and the potential problems a technician may encounter in treating a client if nail trauma or past illness has occurred.

CHAPTER 3

Essential Chemistry of Artificial Nails

INTRODUCTION

Every person who considers themselves to be a professional should strive to be a master of their craft. A nail technician should be skilful at applying nails to all types of nails; they should also be knowledgeable about the products and tools they use. This chapter provides the technician with the basic understanding of the chemicals, chemical processes and generic products that underpin all aspects of artificial nails.

In the nail industry the information available about the products in use tends to be provided from manufacturers of brands and this information is usually tied up with marketing exercises. A technician needs to have the basic knowledge first and the specific product knowledge is then added to this, almost as 'post-graduate' learning.

A good basic understanding of the chemistry involved with artificial nails will help a technician in endless situations. The products may stay the same but the client, their nails and the circumstances and environment will differ every time. By understanding how the chemistry of the products works and what can influence their chemical reactions and performance, the professional technician will be equipped to use all products at their best and solve any problems that may arise.

'SYSTEMS' IN THE NAIL INDUSTRY

Although all types of artificial nails result in either longer or stronger nails that, hopefully, look natural, there are several different methods of achieving these results using different sets of products. These different methods of achieving the same outcome are called 'systems' in the nail industry. The name '**system**' has evolved as a group of specific products working together to produce artificial nails: there is a system of using them together and a chemical system that makes them work.

The three main systems in use

There are three main 'systems' that the industry is familiar with – acrylic, **UV gel** and **fibreglass** – but the names that are in common usage are inaccurate and can be a bit misleading. The inaccuracy of the names of the systems is unimportant as they are widely accepted and understood but an understanding of the underlying chemistry will show the discrepancies. The three main systems have several derivatives that confuse the situation even more, but the different systems refer more to application methods than the system components and chemistry. We can briefly look at each of them.

- **Acrylic**
  This uses a liquid and a powder that, when mixed together, form a solid.
- **UV gel**
  This gel can be called a 'pre-mixed' product that forms a solid when it is exposed to ultraviolet (UV) light.
- **Fibreglass**
  This is a system that utilizes the additional strength of a **fibre** mesh that can be a manmade fibreglass or a natural silk or cotton together with a resin that hardens.

> **TIP**
>
> When learning the skill of artificial nails, it is worth learning one system first until you are confident in all aspects. Additional systems can be added very easily after this until a technician can be classed as 'full service', that is, skilfull in all systems.

The way in which each of these systems works from a chemistry point of view is actually very similar. The application and type of product differs enormously.

When a nail technician starts their career, or is thinking of starting, one of the most confusing and difficult decisions is which system to learn. It is important, in spite of any advice to the contrary, to concentrate on one system at the beginning. The application of artificial nails is a practical skill that needs lots and lots of practice. Experience can be achieved only by working with different clients as this experience cannot be taught. A deep understanding will provide knowledge of how to deal with every situation. While these skills and understanding are being gained as the basis of the profession, it is better to avoid confusing the issue by also trying to understand system differences and characteristics. Once the skills are achieved and the technician has plenty of experience of different situations and problems, it will be a very easy matter to 'add on' another system. In this way the intricacies of the system can be concentrated on, which cannot be done while the basic skills and understanding are still being acquired.

Choosing a system

When choosing which system to learn, there are five main things to take into account:

- **The one you enjoy**. This is the most important. When learning anything new, an enjoyment of the subject or skill will aid learning enormously. There will be one system that an individual will enjoy or find easier that another. The best way of making this decision from an informed point of view is to look at every system, watch their application by an experienced nail technician and, if possible, have a go yourself. A good technician will make every system look incredibly easy, but a few minutes of trying it out will show that none of them is as easy as it looks.

- **Existing confidence and knowledge**. It may be that you have been a client of a technician and have been impressed with the system that has been used. You will also have an amount of knowledge as you have been watching the process. It may be that you already work in a salon and a specific system is used very successfully. These are good reasons for choosing a system but remember that every system is only as good as the technician: every system will work in the correct hands.

- **Financial cost**. Starting any new career or skill can be very expensive. It may be that the cost of a student or starter kit influences this decision. This need not be a problem as the basics are the same for all, and the basic knowledge will provide a good foundation for any system. It is also worth knowing the cost in products for a full set of artificial nails, as this will influence what you can charge your clients for your services.

- **Availability**. Nail products, like hair and beauty products, are available in several ways. There will be one way which suits you better or a combination of several. There are many items that are required for nails, not just the system products, such as cotton wool or nail wipes, disposable towels, terry towels, tools and much more (see Chapter 4). Products are available from direct sales companies that supply them via mail order. Some of these will only sell their products to those who have taken training courses with them or can prove that they are already trained. Others will supply products to anyone. When buying via mail order, you will need to find out what charges are made for postage and packing, if there is a minimum order, how long deliveries take and how payment is made. You will also need to be available to accept delivery of packages. Direct sales companies do not always sell basic items, such as cotton wool, so you will need to go to a wholesaler for these items. If you prefer to see products before you buy, you will need to go to trade shows but not all the direct sales companies attend these shows so you will need to rely on their catalogue.

Another way of buying products is via a wholesaler local to you. There are hundreds of these all over the country and, as they are professional wholesalers, most of them require proof that you are in the trade. Many wholesalers operate a delivery service also and always sell the additional items needed for 'nails'.

What is convenient for you may affect what system you choose. There are many direct sales companies that only sell one system of a specific brand. There are also companies that sell more than one system of specific brands. You may choose the brand rather than the purchase method but take into account what is the most convenient for your situation and how much extra you are prepared to pay (and wait) for delivery or how much time (and petrol) you are prepared to pay for visits to wholesalers.

- **Company advice**. Most product companies are more than willing to give you lots of advice as to what to buy. One word of caution here: the company may advise you that a specific system is the only one for you. This may be the case but if the system is the only one that the company sells there may be another reason why they are promoting it.

As a general piece of advice, do not rush into anything when choosing a system. Do your research, gather information, talk to others, attend trade shows, buy the trade magazines. When you have lots of information you can decide for yourself from an informed position rather than being persuaded by others.

TIP

Accepting that learning the skill of artificial nails is potentially a brand new career and profession will help to accept that sufficient research, learning and practice is essential and will be worth while in the long run.

The chemistry of nail products

The chemistry of nail products for all brands is similar. As beauty therapists who learn how moisturizers work on the skin and how various electrical currents affect tissues, as hairdressers learn how perming solutions curl or straighten hair and hair colours work on the hair, nail technicians need to know how nail products work together and on the nail. Once this is understood, specific product knowledge provided by manufacturers and distributors will enhance skills and understanding and make a better and more professional technician, especially one that has the essential attitude that a technician never stops learning.

When the word '**chemicals**' is mentioned, many people immediately think of danger! This is not so. Everything in the world is made of chemicals, including us! The only exceptions are light and electricity, which are energies that affect chemicals.

Atoms and atomic structures

The smallest state in which a chemical can recognizably exist is an **atom**. This is a microscopic piece of matter that is organized in a way that is specific to the simplest chemicals in existence, that is **elements**. Examples of elements could be oxygen, carbon, hydrogen, calcium; there are over 100 different elements, each with its own kind of atom.

The atomic structure is specific to the different elements but each atom can have a negative or positive charge. As we all know, a negative charge will attract a positive charge and vice versa. When a negative charge is joined to a positive charge a **chemical bond** is created. It is the joining together of these elements in various combinations and configurations that make all the millions of chemicals that make our world.

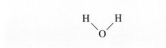

Water H₂O

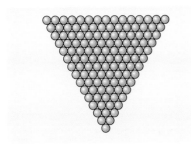

Molecules of water forming a
pyramid of ice

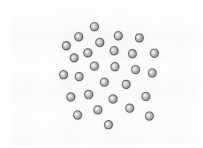

Molecules of water forming liquid
water

Molecules of water forming steam

$$H-\underset{\underset{H}{|}}{\overset{\overset{H}{|}}{C}}-\underset{\underset{H}{|}}{\overset{\overset{H}{|}}{C}}-O-H$$

Ethanol C₂H₅OH

$$H-\underset{\underset{H}{|}}{\overset{\overset{H}{|}}{C}}-C\overset{\diagup H}{\underset{\diagdown O-H}{}}$$

Acetic acid CH₃COOH

Molecules

When an atom joins other atoms it forms a **molecule**. An example of a molecule could be H₂O. The letter H is the symbol for the element hydrogen, the letter O is the symbol for the element oxygen; 2 atoms of hydrogen joined to 1 atom of oxygen makes 1 molecule of water.

This specific molecule is the smallest form in which the chemical known as water can exist. How many molecules there are in a space or how they are joined together determines the form that the water is taking:

- Lots of molecules tightly packed together will be water but in the form of *ice*
- Fewer molecules loosely packed together will be *flowing water*
- Very few molecules with only some packed together will be *steam* (or *vapour*).

Water has the chemical symbol of H₂O but if only one more element is added and the configuration is changed the chemicals that are formed are vastly different from simple water. By adding the element carbon, alcohols (such as the one found in alcoholic drinks: ethanol C₂H₅OH), fatty acids (such as acetic acid in vinegar: CH₃COOH) and even solvents (such as **acetone**, widely used in the nail industry) are formed

We are very familiar with each of these chemicals in their liquid form but are already aware of any possible dangers. Water is quite safe to drink but too much of it in the wrong circumstances is dangerous, we can drown in it. The ethanol in our favourite alcoholic drink is good in small quantities but a bit too much has a very unpleasant effects and a lot too much causes alcoholic poisoning and death. There is no one who would wish to consume too much vinegar and no one who would want acetone in their stomach but we are quite happy to have it remove nail varnish. Chemicals used correctly and in suitable quantities are not dangerous or harmful.

Vapours, fumes and odours

Molecules of chemicals can escape into the air and become **vapours**. Water does not smell but is present in the air all the time. Some chemicals can escape into the air much more easily than others. For example, water under normal conditions does not escape too readily but if left long enough will evaporate. Other types of liquid chemicals, such as **solvents**, can escape very easily and this property is called '**volatile**'. Molecules of the actual chemical are in the air when this happens and they cannot necessarily be detected by smell. These molecules are called vapours as the liquid is vapourizing. Volatile liquids vapourize very easily so should be kept in containers that prevent this. This is particularly relevant to artificial nails, as many products used are volatile chemicals.

The smell of these liquids are often called **fumes**. This is very inaccurate. We refer to car exhaust fumes and this is accurate. These fumes are burned particles in smoke. What is often found in connection to nails is vapour – that is, the volatile chemicals escaping into the air.

Smell or **odour** is another thing again. Some chemicals can be detected by us via our noses. Some chemicals cannot be detected by us via our noses but that does not mean they are not there. A strong smell of nail products would suggest that the chemicals have escaped into the air as vapours which are now being breathed in. (The effects of this will be discussed in Chapter 4.)

Bonding

A basic understanding of how molecules bond together to create something different will be useful in understanding the chemistry of nail systems. It is also important to understand that some molecules will bond together naturally owing to their positive and negative attractions; others need help. The help required could come in the form of heat, light or another chemical to speed up the process. This process is a crucial part in the understanding of nail systems, as the methods used and the speed of reaction affects the results and the application.

Acrylics, polymerization and monomers

Almost every product used in the various nail systems belongs to a vast family of chemicals called 'acrylics'. An acrylic is a manmade type of plastic and those that are used in the nail industry use the same chemical process to form a solid from a liquid or semi-liquid: this process is called '**polymerization**'.

- Polymerization is a process that joins single but complex molecules called monomers together to form a solid even more complex structure called a polymer. The term 'monomer' means 'mono': single + 'mer': unit, 'polymer' means 'poly': many + 'mer': unit. This can be likened in a way to the water molecules discussed earlier. The single molecules can flow around as a liquid; when their temperature is drastically lowered, they join together to form a solid that is ice. It is the lowering of the temperature that has made this happen. (This reaction is not strictly the same as polymerization but thinking of it in this way makes it easier to understand.)
- The monomers are present in some form in all nail system products. As explained, the single units or molecules are

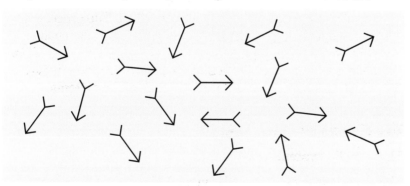

Monomer (liquid)

monomers; there is also a slightly different arrangement where a few units are formed together. These are called '**oligomers**'. As a general rule, the monomers are the products that are liquid in form and the oligomers are in a semi-liquid form, such as a gel or **resin**.

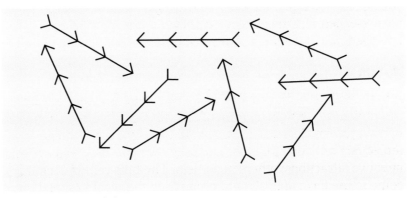

Oligomer (semi-solid)

Thinking back to how proteins are formed, you may remember that amino acids join together in long chains and these chains are linked together by amino acid bonds. These too can be described as polymers as they are single units (the amino acids) joined together to form long chains. Nails are made up of keratin so therefore nails are also polymers.

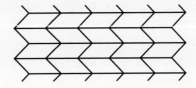

Polymer (solid)

- The cells that are formed in the matrix on the nail unit have in their nucleus (or 'brain') of the cell the instructions to create the keratin. The nucleus initiates the process by collecting the relevant amino acids and causing them to link together in a specific format that will make the protein, keratin. This is the process of polymerization but notice that the instruction from the nucleus was needed to make it happen. To relate this to the nail products is now a simple exercise. The monomers (or oligomers) are present in a nail product. The process is initiated, the single units join together to form long chains with bonds linking them together and a solid is formed. This solid is what creates the artificial nail. The precise way in which this happens is different for each of the systems.

The chemistry of systems

The acrylic system

This system is the most popular in the UK and the US, holding probably about 50 per cent of the nail market. It is also popular in

Europe but other systems hold the largest share in some countries, such as Germany, that favours a UV gel system. The acrylic system was the first to be used commercially, and came, as we saw in Chapter 1, directly from the dental industry. Even the colours that are used came from the dentists as they used pink for dental plates and various shades of white for dentures. (Pink and white is often used to create a natural-looking nail with a white free edge.)

The acrylic system is a two-component system using a liquid monomer and a powder. As already explained, the monomer (liquid) needs to polymerize and become a solid, and it needs the instruction to do this. If a liquid monomer is left exposed to light and at room temperature it would start to polymerize of its own accord, but this reaction would occur very slowly and the resulting polymer would be very soft and jelly-like.

The initiator and the catalyst: The instruction, or **initiator**, must come from somewhere. The solid that is to be formed must also be a strong solid rather than a soft jelly. This is where the powder comes in. The powder in an acrylic is, in fact, tiny polymer beads that have been manufactured to exact specifications. It is the powder that usually carries the initiator that starts the polymerization process.

Two conditions are needed for the process to be successful for the nail industry. An initiator is needed to start the process off and a **catalyst** is needed to determine the speed of the process. These two conditions are created by two different chemicals that, when they come together, start the whole polymerization process and control it. They start the process by giving the monomers a 'blast' of energy. This comes about from the **chemical reaction** that occurs when the two come together – a release of energy that 'kicks' the monomers into linking together.

The two chemicals are like two parts of a whole, and both are essential. The amount of each is also an important factor, as an imbalance or a balance that was created for a different application (such as making dentures) could produce problems. The blast of energy that is produced needs to be controlled, as too much would speed up the process too quickly, not enough would result in a very slow polymerization.

The catalyst process: The most commonly used catalyst system (the two chemicals that start the process) are **benzoyl peroxide** in the powder and an '**amine**' in the liquid. When these two react together they create the 'instruction' for the monomers to join together. A similar reaction is used in permanent or semi-permanent hair dyes. Hydrogen peroxide and amines are used to create the necessary reaction to allow the pigments in the hair dye to enter the hair shaft.

The chemical benzoyl peroxide is commonly used in acne or 'spot' creams that have a medical inference, for example a specific skin condition. It is, however, proving to be problematical as an ingredient in the class of products to which artificial nails belong, cosmetic products. New products are starting to be brought onto the market that do not utilize the same catalyst system and therefore have dispensed with using benzoyl peroxide. However, every acrylic system needs an initiator and catalyst to create the acrylic polymer used for artificial nails.

Acrylic monomer with initiator to 'kick-start' the polymerisation process

+

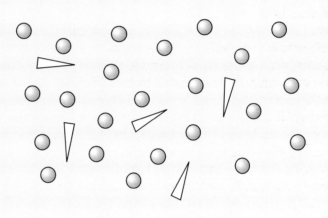

Acrylic polymer powder with catalyst to regulate the speed of the process

=

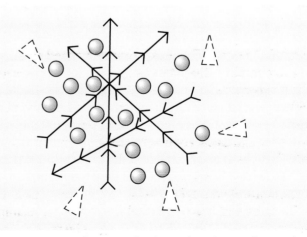

A solid acrylic with polymer chains and polymer beads. Catalyst and initiator used up

The polymer beads: The polymer beads have several roles, including the delivery of the 'instruction' to polymerize. The polymer beads remain as beads during the process and after polymerization is complete. They are in among the long polymer chains that are being formed and give support and strength to the final structure. The monomer alone would produce a soft and flexible structure but, with the polymer beads, the structure can have the flexibility of the monomer together with the strength of the supporting spheres.

The liquid and the powder: The amount of the liquid and powder that is mixed together, that is the 'ratio', is important to the finished solid. Too much powder can make a very hard solid that may be brittle. Too much liquid can result in a soft and weak solid. The correct ratio plays an important role in the performance of the system and needs practice, together with some guidance from the manufacturers.

Another role of the powder is to carry coloured pigment. Technicians and their clients like to have the choice of wearing their artificial nail looking more natural or like a permanent 'French manicure' (with a very white free edge that is often created by nail varnish). This can be achieved by using a pink powder over the nail bed and a white powder on the tip. There are also some powders that provide a colour with a more peach tone for sallow and dark skins. It is possible to use powders that have strong colour pigments designed to take the place of coloured varnish. (If these are used, the whole overlay should be removed every few weeks to make sure that there is not a problem with the natural nail, as this will not be seen through the opaque overlay.)

Methacrylates – EMA and MMA: The chemicals used in this system commonly belong to the methacrylate family. The two most common are **ethyl methacrylate** (or **EMA**) and **methyl methacrylate** (or **MMA**). Both of these were used at one time as monomers, as they were in the dental industry. However, it was discovered that MMA caused a great many allergic reactions and was too aggressive for skin. As a liquid monomer it is now banned in the US although the very low-cost acrylic systems available there are sometimes MMA. MMA is a stronger polymer but, as a monomer, produced very hard and brittle overlays.

EMA is now the most commonly used for monomers. It can cause allergic reactions but by working correctly this should not cause a problem (see Chapter 4). Monomers are a highly reactive substance in that they have a great deal of energy, with the molecules rushing about all over the place. They want to polymerize and, as stated earlier, will do so given enough time. This is one of the reasons why they can cause allergic reactions if they touch the skin too often. When they are polymerized, their energy has gone and it is then less likely to get a reaction to them.

Powders in acrylic nail systems: Powders in this nail system are usually made from the same chemicals as members from the same branch of the same family tree will have very similar characteristics. Powders are already polymers and they can be a 'homopolymer' – that is, it is made from one polymer, either MMA or EMA, or, more usually from two or more polymers, MMA plus EMA, which is called a '**copolymer**'.

EMA will form a softer, more flexible polymer so, when used as a monomer, it needs the strength of a good polymer powder to support it. However, a homopolymer reacts faster with a monomer that is the same. Therefore, an EMA liquid monomer will react faster with an EMA powder polymer, but will produce a relatively soft overlay. An EMA monomer reacts slower with a MMA powder polymer, but can produce a stronger overlay. A regularly used mixture is an EMA monomer with a copolymer of EMA and MMA. This will result in a reasonably fast reaction with a good combination of flexibility and strength.

When a liquid monomer and a powder polymer are mixed together, the resulting product goes through several stages. These stages are 'stage managed' by the catalyst system and the timings of the stages are infinitely variable:

- The first stage when the monomer meets the powder is when the additives to the powder, or beads, are released, which can be called 'swelling'. This is when the reaction really gets going and it happens quite quickly. It can be seen as the product starts to melt.
- The next stage is when the polymerization starts and the mixture stops melting and starts to have more of a gel consistency. At this stage the product can be moved around the nail. The length of this varies in different brands.
- The next stage is when the product leaves the 'gel' stage and goes into the beginning of the final '**cure**' or setting stage. The product cannot be moved around easily now without leaving dips or bumps. Once this stage has been reached, the final cure will not be long. This whole process can take anything from 3 minutes to over 10 minutes and finishes when the product is hard enough to file (or produces a clicking noise when tapped with a brush handle).

    However, do not be fooled! The overlay may be hard enough to file but the polymerization process will continue within it for many hours. Harsh abrasives or hard knocks to the overlay can interfere with this process and create weak areas in the artificial nail.

Temperature and polymerization: There are external factors that can influence the process, the most obvious of which is temperature. A high temperature will speed up the process. Fast polymerization can create a heat sensation on the nail. The process itself produces a small amount of heat as it is an '**exothermic**' reaction (one that gives off heat) but this is too small to be felt by a healthy nail plate under normal circumstances. Fast polymerization can also create a brittle overlay with weak areas. Normal room temperature is ideal, and this is one reason why technicians are not advised to work under desk lamps that get hot.

A low temperature will slow down the polymerization. The result of this can be seen when the liquid monomer is cold or the client's hands are cold. When the overlay is applied crystals or frosting can be seen in the area near the cuticle. This occurs because the process is slow to start and the volatile monomer is evaporating leaving some of the powder on the nail. This can be avoided by using the monomer at room temperature and keeping your client's hands warm.

When the chemical engineering is unbalanced: The acrylic nail system, as can be seen, is a delicately balanced piece of chemical engineering. Several things can change this balance. The addition of extra chemicals, for example, can have disastrous results. The most common addition of other chemicals is the use of a brush cleaner (see Chapter 4).

The traditional acrylic system (with benzoyl peroxide as a catalyst system) is prone to discoloration, or yellowing, caused by ultraviolet light from either the sun or sunbeds. Some brands of the system have an additive that prevents this type of discoloration by working in a way that is similar to sunscreens for the skin. Some have a blue or violet colour added to the liquid. This is present as an **optical brightener**, to make the white look whiter and the pink look pinker, but it will also cover any slight yellowing.

Some brands of the system require the application of a **UV block**, in the form of a varnish, over the finished nail. This type needs the block to be reapplied regularly. The acrylic systems that do not use benzoyl peroxide do not have this problem of discoloration. However, all brands are prone to discoloration owing to contamination, which is dealt with in Chapter 6.

The chemical balance in this system is crucial to its performance. It is very ill-advised to mix brands – that is, a liquid monomer of one type with a powder from another. The catalyst system may not be compatible and other additives may not work together. Always use a system that is designed to be used together.

The UV gel system

This system is sometimes called a 'pre-mixed' system, as it does not need another product or chemical for it to work. What it does need, however, is ultraviolet light to make it cure, or set. Like the acrylic system, it has, in the most part, been derived from the dental industry that uses light-cured materials to seal teeth.

The initiator and the catalyst: Like the acrylic system, the semi-liquid gel that is applied to the nails needs to polymerize or cure. The acrylic system uses a catalyst system that initiates the process with a blast of energy. The energy needed to start the polymerization process in this system is ultraviolet light. Light, as we have seen earlier, is a form of energy as is electricity and heat.

You may remember learning about light from your school days. Light energy comes from either the sun, or electrical energy is converted into light. In the visible light spectrum – that is, light that we can see – there is ultraviolet at one end and infra red at the other. In the spectrum outside this central band are energies such as microwaves, X rays and radio waves.

Ultraviolet light: There has been some concern about using ultraviolet light in a nail system, as it is perceived as being harmful. Ultraviolet light can be very harmful, but in the case of nail systems this is not the case. There are three different 'strengths' or wavelengths of ultraviolet light: UVA, UVB and UVC. All of these are emitted from the sun in various amounts. When getting a tanned skin from the sun or a sunbed, the skin produces a pigment called melanin that protects the underlying tissues from the harmful effects of the dangerous wavelengths of ultraviolet light. This process needs relatively large quantities of UVA, which is safe, and smaller quantities of UVB, which can be harmful. In sunbed tubes, the percentages of these two wavelengths are such that the process of melanin production will work without being harmful (unless exposure to the light exceeds safe levels for the individual). 'Fast-tan' sunbeds sometimes have a higher percentage of UVB to speed up the process. The size of these tubes are usually 100 watts and an average sunbed has about 24 such tubes: a blast of 2400 watts of UV light!

The story is different for nail systems. The tubes in most nail lamps emit only UVA, it is not necessary to have UVB. Tubes are usually 6 or 9 watts and lamps can have from 1 to 5 tubes, depending on the design. The maximum 'blast' is therefore only 45 watts of UVA.

It is worth remembering these brief facts in case your client asks, 'Will my fingers get a tan?' or 'Is the UV light harmful?'

UV gel, oligomers and polymerization: So now we understand a bit about UV energy, how does it affect the UV gel? All the nail systems need some form of energy to make them a solid structure on the nail. An acrylic system needs the energy generated from a chemical reaction. UV gel needs UV energy to turn it from a semi-liquid into a solid. The process of forming a solid, as with all other systems, is called polymerization.

- The gel used in this system varies throughout the brands but all are from the acrylic family. The liquid in the acrylic system has single units of monomer, hence the liquid form. Gels have short chains of units, called oligomers, that are not long enough to be called a polymer. This gives the gel its consistency and makes the creation of polymers from light energy easier as they are partially formed already.
- When a UV gel is subjected to the energy of ultraviolet light, the polymerization process starts and continues in much the same way as with acrylics. Like acrylics, the process is exothermic – that is, the chemical reaction gives off heat.

This is relatively easy to control with acrylics as it is the carefully balanced chemistry that does most of the controlling. This is not always the case with UV gels as there are many variables that can cause a much stronger exothermic reaction.

- When a blast of energy is applied to the oligomers they literally rush around at great speed, linking up with each other. All this rushing about creates a heat that is a bit like friction caused by rubbing two things together: the faster the rubbing, the greater the heat. This happens in the gel if the energy blast is too high, if the output of the UV lamp is too high for the specific gel – for example, a lamp with a 45 watt output may be too strong for a gel that is designed for a lamp that has only a 9 watt output. It can also happen if the layer of gel is very thick. This is because there are more oligomers rushing around in a greater space and creating the friction effect. (To put this picture into perspective: if the nail was the size of the UK, the oligomer would be about the size of an ant!)

- This excess heat is a problem, for two reasons. The first is because the heat can be so great that it is felt by the nerve endings in the nail bed and the pain can be very severe and very frightening. This is obviously unpleasant for the client and it can damage the nail bed. Some clients are more prone to feeling this heat sensation than others and the nail bed will be particularly sensitive if it is damaged or thinned owing to excess buffing. The second problem is that such a fast polymerization will create a very brittle polymer that could easily crack or shatter. It can be avoided by using the correct UV lamp and avoiding thick layers of a gel that is not designed for this type of application. (Always follow the manufacturer's instructions.)

UV gel and oxygen: Polymerization does not like oxygen! The presence of oxygen slows down, or *inhibits*, the process. This is the case with polymerization in the acrylic system, too, but the method is not so sensitive to it. Gel, however, is sensitive to oxygen. There are many gels available on the market that, when cured under the UV lamp, still have a sticky surface. There have been stories that this happens because the gel cures from the bottom up and liquid is pushed up to the surface, and various others. The truth is due to the role oxygen plays in its hinderance of the process. Oxygen is all around us in the air; the surface of the gel is exposed to oxygen and therefore does not polymerize as the oxygen is inhibiting the process.

This sticky layer is not a problem if is removed correctly and thoroughly. It is the oligomers that are not polymerized and, like the liquid monomer in the acrylic system, are likely to cause allergic reactions if the skin is touched. There are some gels on the market that do not have this sticky layer. This is owing to a total cure where the problem of oxygen inhibition has been solved.

Viscosities of gels: The chemical make up of the gels is very complicated and the different types of gel that are available all have differences in both their make up and characteristics. One of the first things that can be seen about the gels is the thickness of each of them. This thickness is called '**viscosity**'. A thick liquid is described as viscous; water or any liquid that is free flowing has a very low viscosity.

Gels, depending on their purpose and depending on the manufacturer, are available in various viscosities. The low-viscosity gels are used for painting thin layers onto nails and building up a sufficient coating to strengthen the natural or artificial nail. They are also used, depending on their characteristics, as a finishing layer that has a very high-gloss shine.

Thicker, or more viscous gels, are applied in fewer layers and again, depending on their characteristics, can be applied to create a specific structure to provide maximum strength to the nail. Some gels do not hold their shape for long before curing and care must be taken to avoid the gel running into the sides of the nail and onto the skin. Other types of thicker gels do hold their shape and stay where they are placed. These, however, have a consistency that is similar to petroleum jelly and can be difficult to apply without plenty of practice.

Shrinkage of UV gel: Polymerization of any kind is prone to some shrinkage as the chains form. Gel is particularly prone to this and, if the shrinkage is severe, the overlay will lift from the nail plate or the client may feel a tightness that can make the finger tip throb. A good-quality gel should not shrink too much, but thicker layers will shrink more than thinner ones.

'American' and 'European' gel: There are two distinct types of UV gel on the market. They are often known as an 'American' gel and a 'European' gel. Every gel will have different characteristics and every manufacturer will have created a specific formula.

TIP

These gels tend to be affected by temperature. A cold gel will be very viscous (thick); a warm gel will have a thin consistency. A thick gel will warm up when applied to a nail and become more runny. This should be allowed for when using these products.

- As a very general description of the 'American' type of gels, they are based on epoxy and urethane acrylate oligomers. Although the viscosities can vary enormously, they tend to be self-levelling so can usually be used only in thin layers as thicker layers would run into the side walls and cuticles. They are usually very resistant to solvents so will keep their shine through many changes of nail varnish colour but cannot be removed easily with solvents.
- The type of gel that is sometimes known as the 'European' gel also usually has urethane **acrylates** plus esters of acrylic. The style of gel in this category often has a component system that uses more than one type of gel. The components may have a bonder gel that will make sure the gel does not lift from the nail plate, a building or sculpting gel and a sealer gel. There could also be a gel that can be used alone to build in thinner layers like the 'American' gel. The main gel will have a much higher viscosity and a creamier consistency. When applied, the gel will tend to stay in place and not run.

The fibreglass system

Rather than from the dental industry, this system has developed from the beauty industry! Before artificial nails and all the accompanying products, manicurists developed a method of repairing split nails. It involved tissue paper and clear varnish. A split in the nail was sealed by painting the nail with a clear varnish then applying a small piece of tissue paper to hold the split together and then painting several layers of clear varnish over the top to give it strength and a smooth finish. This method could work but was not always satisfactory as it was not very strong, could peel off and came off with nail varnish remover. If the split was close to the end of the nail, however, it could be saved temporarily until it could be filed away.

Stick-on nails were introduced into both the retail market and professional market where a whole plastic nail was attached with a strong glue over the natural nail. These **glues** or adhesives were useful to repair natural nails and also stick the paper used to hold the edges together.

The three-component system: This could be called a three-component system, because there are three products necessary within the system – **fabric mesh**, **resin** and a **resin activator**.

- **Fabric mesh**: As the name of the system suggests, a fabric is used to provide a cross-linked structure and give the overlay strength (a bit like the polymer beads in the acrylic system). Any thin fabric will work, but those in common use and produced specifically for the job are a fibreglass mesh and a natural silk. These are both a fine mesh with a sticky back, and are used to reinforce the overlay. The one you use is a matter of personal preference.
  - *Fibreglass* is, as the name suggests, fibres with a high glass content. Out of the two, this is slightly stronger as the glass remains untouched by the resin, as a linked structure. It is more difficult to 'wet' than silk.
  - *China silk* is a very fine mesh of natural silk fibres. It does reinforce the structure but the resin soaks into the fibres, unlike the fibreglass, and the silk becomes an integral part of the resin. It is easier to 'wet' than fibreglass.

  The mesh comes in strips that is cut, using special scissors, to the width of the nail, or in pre-cut 'fingers'.
- **Resin**: The second component of this system is a resin. This, again belongs to the acrylic family of chemicals and is a **cyanoacrylate** of a specific chemical structure and viscosity. It is used to 'wet' the fibre so that it cannot be seen and then build up to an overlay. Cyanoacrylate is a monomer like the other systems but has a different chemical structure. It is sensitive to air and moisture and will cure (polymerize) when exposed to either.

  Cyanoacrylates are used in a great many industries as an adhesive, in the motor industry, plumbing, wood working and many others including the medical industry, where it can be used as a skin or bone adhesive. Obviously, there are different kinds of this adhesive and different grades or qualities. The type most suitable for nails is an **ethyl cyanoacrylate**. The viscosity is infinitely variable, as is the speed at which it cures. A high-grade cyanoacrylate is also preferable. This chemical is used as an adhesive for nail tips but a specific viscosity and chemical make-up is called a resin and is used in this nail system.

- **Resin activator**: The resin will set or cure, in time, on its own, as it uses moisture from the air to set. As this takes at least 15 minutes and results in a very pliable coating that can peel off easily, it is not practical for the technician. To speed up the process and produce a strong overlay, an activator is used. The activator is usually an alcohol-based product, or an alkaline, of a dilution that will cause a controlled set.

Polymerization: As with the other nail systems, this system is based on acrylic polymers. When the resin is polymerized, it forms long chains but does not have any **cross-links** and needs the added strength of a fibre mesh. Owing to the lack of cross-links, it needs special care when removing nail varnish or using household cleaners.

The process of polymerization, as we know, gives off energy in the form of heat. When the process is properly controlled at the right speed, this heat cannot be felt. If the process occurs too quickly then excessive heat is produced, which can be very uncomfortable for the client and produce a weak overlay.

By applying the resin and spraying it with activator, the polymerization process is started as the reaction is given the blast of energy required. To control the speed of the process, a very small amount of activator should be sprayed from a distance of approximately 12 inches. If the client feels any heat at all, the spray is too close. A fast cure is not only uncomfortable, it also produces a brittle and cloudy overlay that has thousands of tiny cracks.

Fibre mesh: When introducing the fibre mesh into this system, it is important that the mesh is not visible through the overlay. To make it invisible it needs to be '**wetted**'. This is the term used to describe the application of resin to the fibre to make sure it penetrates the mesh and makes it invisible. It is essential that this is done with care as an artificial nail with the fibre showing through does not look natural. The mesh needs soaking with the resin before any further layers are applied. (This method is described in Chapter 6.)

OTHER IMPORTANT CHEMICAL REACTIONS IN NAIL SYSTEMS

Tip adhesives

There are other chemical reactions that we need to understand. One of them is closely associated with the fibreglass system as it involves cyanoacrylates. This is the tip adhesives. Tip adhesives are almost always an ethyl cyanoacrylate that is sensitive to moisture and whose cure is inhibited by oxygen. The viscosities can vary from a water-like liquid to a thick gel. As a general rule, the thicker the adhesive, the slower the cure, and variations will apply to personal preference and also the job in hand.

- Tip adhesives, as the name implies, are used to stick a plastic tip to the natural nail. As the adhesive is sandwiched between the tip and the nail, the oxygen is expelled (therefore no inhibition to the cure) and there is sufficient moisture in the nail to encourage the polymerization. The thin adhesives cure very quickly, in a couple of seconds, the thicker ones take a little longer.
- Personal preference depends on how quickly the technician wants the tip to stick firmly. Beginners tend to prefer to have a bit longer to position the tip before it is too late, experienced technicians like to work as fast as possible. However, speed is not always the main consideration. A thin adhesive can produce only a thin layer of adhesive between the tip and nail. This is fine if the tip fits the nail exactly and the nail plate does not have any irregularities. If this is not the case, air pockets are created that not only look bad but can also create problems later. A thicker adhesive can form a thicker layer and fill up any irregularities. The gel-like adhesives are an invaluable help when dealing with a severe nail biter or a nail shape that tilts upward as the spaces can be safely filled with adhesive (see Chapter 6).
- Cyanoacrylate adhesives can, over time, break down in water so, in the artificial nail you should not put too much confidence in the bond between the tip and the nail for strength. The strength needs to be between the overlay and the nail.

Primers

Function of a primer

There are some brands that do not require any help for the overlay to bond to the natural nail. They may just need a very clean, oil-free surface that has had the shine removed. Some systems have a built-in method of bonding a manmade plastic to a natural surface of keratin. The majority need some help to create this bond and the general name of the product that is used is called a '**primer**'. The equivalent of primers are seen in many areas: metal needs a metal primer before it can be painted, as do ceramic tiles; wood needs an undercoat; natural nails should have a base coat before varnishing; even teeth need a primer before a veneer can be applied. A primer is needed in these cases as whatever is being applied to the surface needs to bond with it, otherwise it will peel or fall off.

A primer prepares the surface to accept a substance that does not naturally bond with it. Shiny surfaces do not bond together easily and a roughened surface will accept another substance more readily. Nails, when shiny, almost have a seal on the surface that prevents too much penetration of substances. When this shine is removed, the surface more readily bonds with adhesive or overlays and it also allows a small amount to penetrate and create a stronger bond.

Methacrylic acid

Some nail systems require extra help in the form of a separate primer. The most common primer in use is a chemical called **methacrylic acid**. As can be seen from the name, it again belongs to the acrylic family and therefore will have an affinity to the overlay. The acid part of it, although mild, will gently etch the surface of the nail and encourage it to accept the overlay. It forms both a chemical and mechanical bond by holding the overlay onto the nail plate.

Methacrylic acid is a strong irritant and is corrosive. Care must be taken when using it not to allow it to touch any soft tissue. Bottles must be kept with the lid on and spillages dealt with with care.

Acid-free primers

There are some other types of primers available and these are generally called 'acid-free'. They will work in such a way as to hold onto the natural nail and hold onto the overlay. They 'interface', or soak into, the nail plate and, as a type of monomer, will polymerize with the overlay to create a complete structure.

The best primer to use is the one that is recommended by the manufacturer as they will have developed it to give the best results with their system. As with all nail systems, information on the products and how to use them efficiently and safely must come from the manufacturer. A technician should spend some time learning, in depth, all there is to know about the products and a reputable company will provide this knowledge. There may also be some application techniques that are best to use with specific brands that make application quicker or more affective. Do not consider that such training is a waste of money or time, it is the complete opposite. Every product on the market will work efficiently in the right hands. In the wrong hands that do not have sufficient knowledge, most products will not 'work'.

ARTIFICIAL NAIL REMOVAL

A final explanation of the chemistry of artificial nails is their removal. The most commonly used method of removal is to soak the nails in acetone or another solvent. The solvent does not dissolve the overlay but breaks down the bonds between the polymer chains. The stronger the bonds, the more difficult it is to break them down.

Using a solvent

In the various systems, the cyanoacrylate resin in the fibreglass system has the weakest bonds as there are no cross-links in the structure. UV gel is usually the most difficult to remove as the bonds are exceptionally strong. There are many gels that cannot be removed with solvents, and the only way is to buff them off.

When the nails are soaked in the solvent, the bonds break down and the structure becomes soft. While in the solvent, the overlay can be scraped off quite easily. If the nails are removed from the solvent before this is done, the softened acrylic immediately becomes hard again.

In order to understand what happens to the acrylic in the solvent, imagine putting paper in water (those with children may have needed to fish out a roll of toilet paper from the lavatory in the past!). The paper becomes very soft and liable to break up. It is still, however, paper and does not dissolve in the water. When it is removed from the water and dries out, it may feel a little harder and the separate sheets may have moulded together but it is still paper. This is very similar to the effect acetone has on acrylic nails.

The use of acetone

There have been some worries about using acetone to remove artificial nails. All solvents are classed as hazardous chemicals and all chemicals, even water, are potentially hazardous if care is not taken in their use and storage. Overuse of any hazardous chemical is a danger but sensible use should not be a problem. The skin continually soaking in acetone or any other solvent could cause health problems but there should be no need to keep removing artificial nails. The only reasons to do so would be if a problem with the natural nail or skin was suspected or the client decides that they no longer want or need them. Correctly maintained artificial nails do not need removing. Occasional removal by soaking in acetone or similar solvent is not a problem as long as the correct procedures are followed and used solvents are disposed of carefully.

SUMMARY

This chapter has explored the chemical reactions that underpin the three main 'systems' – acrylic, UV gel and fibreglass – used in artificial nail technology, and what the choice of system entails for both technician and client.

CHAPTER 4

Preparing the Work Area

INTRODUCTION

The only way to provide professional nail treatments is in a suitable, comfortable and safe environment with the right tools correctly used. This chapter will show how to create that environment, make it safe for both the technician and client and how to keep it that way while abiding by the relevant legislation.

Starting with the general environment, we need to think about what area is needed for a nail technician to work, what is required within the salon and what problems need addressing that are specific to artificial nails.

EQUIPMENT

Whether the technician is working in a nail salon, a beauty salon or a hair salon, a minimum space is needed. In comparison to the other services, the space needed is very small. This industry has a great many mobile technicians working in it; virtually all of the requirements that make a salon a safe, hygienic and comfortable place also apply to working as a mobile technician. The only difference is that tools, equipment and products need to be portable. As clients are still central to the work, all the safety rules must still apply.

The desk

In thinking about the minimum space required for a technician, a desk is the first consideration. There are many nail desks available from wholesalers that have been specifically designed for the job. If space is at a premium then the minimum work top would need to be approximately 75 cm wide and approximately 35 cm deep. Ideally, the desk should have a couple of drawers, and be very stable in construction. The width of the desk should be not so wide that the technician needs to stretch to reach the client's hands if the client is sitting back in the chair, nor should it be so narrow that it causes the technician to bend their neck down too far.

Before buying a ready-made desk, make sure the measurements are right for the space in the salon; sit in the chair that is going to be used for both the technician and the client. Think about storage of all the equipment needed and, if necessary, the space required for any additional storage needs. Most ready-made desks usually have a suitable work top that can be kept clean easily, but remember to take that into consideration.

Many salons have their desks made specially to match the image of the salon. It is possible to make a functional desk fit in with any décor but remember that the suitability and safety of the desk and chairs must come before image. Think of the essential requirements first and design the desk around them, rather than thinking of the design first and trying to make it work.

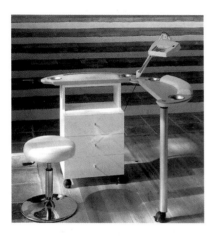

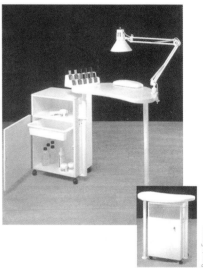

A selection of available desks

The technician's chair

Around the desk should be sufficient room for a comfortable chair for the technician and their client. Care should be taken when choosing the technician's chair, as there are several factors to take into account:

- A busy technician can be sitting in the same place for, sometimes, up to 12 hours a day with very few breaks. This is far from an ideal situation but most salons have at least one late night.
- As with any work equipment, safety must come first. A chair must have the correct support for the user. The seat should be padded and of a depth that supports the legs. The tilt of the seat also affects how we sit. The back rest should give support to the back and the combination of the back and seat should encourage the user to sit upright with a slight hollow in the lower back. Technicians are forced to work in a very unnatural position, leaning forward and with the head looking down. This puts great strain on the back and neck. Every technician should be aware that this position causes stress in the neck and shoulders and could give severe problems in later years.
- Many technicians work by leaning one elbow on the desk and their body twisted. This is obviously very dangerous. The

Technician's chair

upper body needs to be square to the desk with the back straight and only a slight tilt forward. The shoulders should be kept relaxed and the neck should not be held bent too much. There are 'posture' chairs available on wheels and with a rocking motion that is designed to help those working on a desk. These chairs have a tilted seat and a padded place for the knees to rest. They are ideal for the person who sits upright all the time, such as a typist, or the person who needs to lean forward slightly, as they will keep the curvature of the back in the correct position. However, owing to the nature of the technician's work a lot of pressure is put on the knees in this position and this can be quite painful at the end of a day and will cause problems later.

- There are several exercises that a technician can do at various times throughout the day, but, at all times sitting in the safest position and keeping relaxed is essential advice.

The client's chair

The chair for the client is almost as important:

- The client must feel comfortable but must also be in the right position for the technician. A client could spend up to 2 hours in the same chair so comfort is important. A fabric-covered chair with a soft seat is preferable (plastic can get uncomfortable). The height of the seat should be such that the client can rest their arms on the desk easily while keeping them relaxed and shoulders in a relaxed position. They should also be able to get close enough to the desk so that their arm is still supported if they lean back into the chair.
- When seating a client and during the whole treatment, the client must sit straight in front of the desk. This is important for the treatment as if a client is sitting sideways their hand will not be in the centre and straight to the technician. This could result in artificial nails being applied unevenly on the finger.

It is worth aquiring the very best furniture that you can afford at the time. It is often a false economy to buy things cheaply thinking that they can be replaced soon. What usually happens is that the cheap items wear out and become tatty very quickly and there is always some other priority that needs the money spending on it. If space in the salon is not at a premium, it is often worth having a much larger desk than necessary (as long as it is not just extra room to clutter and make untidy!) as small displays can be put on the extra top space. There are many inventive technicians that have designed wonderful desks with display areas, built-in waste disposal and multiple desks.

The desk lamp

Desk lamps play a very important part in the work of the technician and their desk set up. It is essential to have excellent light when providing any nail treatment so a lamp of the right design is important. Good light is needed for the technician to avoid eye strain while carrying out close work; direct light, rather than that which has shadows, is needed to examine artificial nails for imperfections; applying varnish and nail art needs bright light to ensure accuracy and neatness.

Lamps are visually very obvious on a desk so need to look pleasing and fit in with the décor of the salon. More importantly, there are several factors that need to be taken into account when choosing a lamp.

Heat

One of the most important is that of heat. Commonly used tungsten bulbs give off a great deal of heat. 'Daylight' bulbs, useful for keeping colours true, also get very hot. This is far from ideal for the technician. The lamp needs to be quite close for the best effect but the working temperature for the technician can get very uncomfortable. The heat will also affect many artificial nail products and make working with them difficult. The heat will also cause volatile products, such as nail varnish remover and liquid monomers, to evaporate faster, creating a potentially high concentration of them in the air space around the technician and client.

Shape

The shape of the lamp needs to be such that the light does not glare into the eyes of either the technician or client; it needs to be close enough to be effective but not in the way; it also needs to be stable on the desk.

Electricity supply

Thought needs to be given to the electricity supply for the lamp. Trailing wires in a workplace are a safety hazard and must be avoided. A socket close enough to avoid trailing wires is the most suitable but there are many alternatives. Some designs of manicure tables have a plug socket already attached to them for electric equipment. This still needs to be connected to an electricity supply and, again, wires across the floor must be avoided. If there is no alternative to a wire on the floor by a desk or any area where people could walk, then it must be covered with a rubber conduit that draws attention to it and has sloping sides to prevent tripping while protecting the cable from damage. There should be no wires under the desk on the floor as the wheels of the chair could run over them, damage them or pull off the equipment. Wherever possible, wires and cables should be attached to the desk, floor or wall using the clips designed for the job that are readily available from any DIY store.

Remember, 'nails' are part of the image industries so make sure you give the right image to your clients.

HEALTH AND SAFETY
Trailing wires are a hazard!

USING NAIL PRODUCTS SAFELY

Problems with irritants and corrosive materials

The majority of nail products come under the category of hazardous chemicals and many of them are classed as irritants. Care *must* be taken when using these types of products. There are some irritants that are also classed as **corrosive** and these will react with everyone. A day-to-day example of this would be household bleach that stings and itches on contact with skin.

> **HEALTH AND SAFETY**
> You are working with hazardous substances – handle and store with care!

- A common example of this type of chemical in the nail industry would be an acid-based primer. This is a product commonly used in artificial nail systems and, as the name suggests, is an acid that will sting and itch on contact with skin. Washing in running water will remove the chemical but it is likely that the skin will be temporarily damaged.
- Many other commonly used products are **irritants** – for example, nail adhesive that is available as professional and retail products is an irritant, and every bottle and tube should carry a warning. Obviously the adhesive will bond skin very easily but a drop of it spilled onto skin will also cause a chemical burn. (Water will stop the burning and acetone will debond the skin.)
- Warnings are carried on many labels following legal requirements, but the absence of warnings does not mean the product is safe. All products should be treated with respect and all potentially hazardous products should have a document called the Material Safety Data Sheet (MSDS) available (see below).

Allergies and sensitivity

All chemicals are potentially harmful but the dividing line that makes a chemical safe and harmful is the *quantity* of it. This dividing line varies from person to person. When a harmful chemical touches the body in any way, the body reacts to it. This reaction can take many different forms but the commonest is an allergic reaction.

- People develop an allergy or sensitivity to a substance by coming into contact with too much of it. It is this level of 'too much' that is so variable. One individual may become sensitive to a particular ingredient in a hand cream after two uses; another may take years before a reaction occurs, if one occurs at all.
- As many nail products are classed as irritants, it is very likely that most individuals will develop a sensitivity to them at some time. As no one can tell how long this will take or how much a specific product needs to come into contact with a person, it is important to take measures to avoid the possibility of a sensitivity building up. It is also just as important to be able to recognize the first signs of this in both the technician and their clients (see Chapter 3).

Absorption, ingestion and inhalation

There are three ways potentially harmful chemicals can enter the body and if each of these 'routes of entry' is prevented as far as possible, all hazards are avoided. The 'routes' are:

- **Inhalation**: that is, *breathing in* vapours or dusts. This one is not so easy to control, but by following strict working practices and hygiene rules, the problem can be solved.
- **Ingestion**: that is, *through the mouth*. Avoidance of this is even easier! Wash hands frequently, especially before eating, do not eat or drink at a desk and follow reasonable salon hygiene rules.
- **Absorption**: that is, chemicals can enter *through the skin*. This is probably the most common cause of problems for technicians and their clients and can be easily avoided.

We will look at all three in more detail.

Inhalation

Thinking of the salon environment and what type of salon it is, there are certain requirements for the safety and comfort of staff and clients.

Vapours

- Many of nail products involve *volatile chemicals* and even the tidiest technician cannot totally prevent some of the vapours escaping into the air. Adequate **ventilation** is essential. In a very busy nail salon a sophisticated ventilation system would be ideal but this arrangement can cost a great deal of money and is not always necessary for smaller establishments with a few nail desks. For the larger salons that need suitable ventilation, expert advise should be sought as there are mathematical formulas that can indicate what size and type of ventilation equipment is needed to change the air in the salon several times an hour.
- Remembering what was explained in Chapter 3, vapours are *molecules of the actual chemical in the air* and, although most nail products have strong odours, if they are not obvious it does not mean they are not there. Not all hazardous chemicals have odours that can be detected. A fan in the salon has no affect on ventilation, all it does is move the air around. The salon needs the air to be changed regularly, and this can be done only by real ventilation. Extractor fans can be suitable and are relatively inexpensive, but they must either be big enough or there must be enough of them and they must be in the right position to be effective.
- The vapours that need to be eliminated are always *heavier than air* so the molecules will not rise very high but will collect nearer the floor. High-level extractors, if a sufficient size for the room, will in theory lift the vapours up and expel them. However, in doing that, the air is being brought up past

the breathing spaces of those in the salon so some of the vapours will be inhaled. Vapours will also be left at the lower levels. Extractors that are set lower down will remove the vapours without having to lift them up.

- Some nail products are used as a *spray*. This is an obvious potential hazard as the chemical is actually being put into the air. Pump sprays are less harmful as they produce larger droplets rather than a fine **mist**. Keep sprays to a minimum, but if they are used, good ventilation is essential.
- Wearing a *disposable dust mask* will not protect anyone from vapours. Chemical molecules that are present in the air are much smaller than dust particles and the mask is not a barrier to them. There are vapour masks available but these are much larger pieces of equipment and are costly to buy. They are also very off-putting to clients!
- Safe, hygienic and correct working procedures will avoid almost all vapours escaping in the air and, in a small to medium salon, this together with adequate ventilation from an open window or door, should be sufficient to ensure safety.

Vapours and eyes

HEALTH AND SAFETY
Always change your contact lenses for glasses before you start to treat a client

- **Contact lenses**: *Never* wear contact lenses when working with nail products. It is possible that vapours can be absorbed in soft lenses and seriously affect the eye. Safety glasses worn with lenses are not good enough.
- **Safety glasses**: Wearing plain safety glasses is highly recommended. It is a practice with some technicians to nip off old overlay, a practice that is very strongly discouraged as it severely damages the nail plate; chips from this can fly and enter the eye. But eye accidents can also happen with the most careful technician, by clipping a plastic tip or nail, or opening a bottle of adhesive that has an air bubble in the nozzle, for example. A busy technician spends many hours very close to a number of hazards and eyes are very precious!

Keeping vapours to a minimum

There are simple rules that can be followed to keep vapours to a minimum:

- Keep *all* bottles and jars closed
- Keep any dishes covered
- Have a metal waste bin with a lid at every desk
- Put all nail wipes/cotton wool straight into the bin after use
- Change the paper towel under the hands after each stage and put into the bin
- Wipe up spills immediately with absorbant paper and put paper in an outside waste bin
- When using a solvent to remove artificial nails, keep the bowl covered with a towel and remove directly after use
- Keep the use of sprays to a minimum
- Discard all unwanted solvents and nail monomers immediately by soaking in absorbant paper and placing in a

covered waste bin; larger quantities should be placed in a safe place in the open and allowed to evaporate – *do not* pour down sinks or lavatories

- Store brushes in covered containers, not open on the desk
- Maintain adequate ventilation at all times, and make sure the salon is not too hot.

TIP

In larger salons it may be worth having a large glass jar with a metal mesh across the top. Volatile liquids can be placed in this and allowed to evaporate in the open air outside the salon in a safe place. Do not place the jar where smoking is allowed and do not use it for more than $1/2$ litre. Larger quantities need to be disposed of safely by a local authority or private disposal means.

Dust

Dust is another major problem in the salon. Although the amount of dust can be minimized by correct working procedures, it is impossible to avoid the production of quantities of dust.

- Dust falls into two categories: the dust you can see and the dust you cannot see. All dust is potentially harmful but the dust you can see is slightly less harmful that the dust you cannot see. Larger dust particles will settle on surfaces and not float around in the air to be breathed in. The body has some very clever mechanisms to prevent unwanted 'foreign matter' entering it. Inhalation is one of the main entry points of the body (ingestion via the mouth and absorption through the skin being the other two, see later). Our respiratory system is designed to take air in through the nose and out through the mouth. The nose has thousands of hairs and is lined with a mucous membrane, both of which are there to trap particles that must not be breathed into the lungs.
- This safety mechanism is very efficient in catching the dust particles that can be seen. It is not as efficient at catching the particles that cannot be seen as they can be so small that they can be inhaled right into the lungs. The mucous membranes of the lungs will catch a great deal of the inhaled dust but it is an irritant and excess dust can cause respiratory problems.

Avoiding excess dust

Like any potential risk situation, it is far better to try to avoid it than correct or treat any problems that arise. There are a number of ways that excess dust can be avoided

- The ideal arrangement is to have a *dust extractor* fitted into the desk. These units, like extractor fans, create a light suction that draws the dust being generated from filing through a grille in the desk top and into a collection bag or unit, rather like a vacuum bag. This collected dust can then be regularly disposed of; an efficient unit can remove almost all the dust before it disperses in the air. The grille need be exposed only during the stages that generate dust; otherwise it can be covered with a manicure mat and towels for the comfort of the client and hygiene of the salon.
- If this type of extractor is not possible, the following suggestions should help to cut down dust:
  – Lay several sheets of disposable towels over a terry towel before each client arrives. After each stage of treatment that

HEALTH AND SAFETY
Try always to use procedures that minimize dust

generates any dust, fold the top layer and discard. This ensures that dust is not left lying under your hands and being continually disturbed.

– Wipe desk surface after each client with a *damp* cloth to collect any dust. This is also the ideal time to use a hard-surface disinfectant to dampen the cloth.

– Wipe all surfaces in the salon with a damp cloth every day. Dusting with a dry cloth will just 'rearrange' the dust.

– Keep air moving with adequate ventilation via windows and doors, which will help remove fine airborne dust.

– Brushing reusable files and buffers to remove dust will lengthen their life. Brush them under running water before disinfecting them.

– Buffers and files should not be used for more than one client without disinfecting. Put used files in a covered box until the cleaning process as they will 'shed' dust wherever they are put down.

Dust masks

For those technicians who feel susceptible to dust a disposable mask can be worn. They are comfortable to wear and should be changed every few days. It is unlikely that any client would need to wear a mask as they are exposed to the dust for a very short space of time. A technician, however, is working in the same environment all day. A technician who wears a mask should explain this to all clients in case they feel at risk.

Drills

The use of drills is not recommended in this book. Modern products and techniques do not require the use of drills, unlike the old, thick and brittle dental acrylics that took hours to buff. Good application techniques should negate the effectiveness of drills. If a technician chooses to use a drill then a course of practical tuition must be taken to fully understand the correct use of the equipment. It should also be understood that drills create huge quantities of very fine dust. Anyone using a drill *must* wear a dust mask for their own safety and follow stringent rules for the management of the dust.

Ingestion

Obviously, technicians do not make a habit of eating or drinking any of their nail products! It is, however, exactly what does happen in a great number of salons by hundreds of technicians. Every time there is a coffee cup on the desk, every time a technician grabs a quick bite of their lunchtime sandwich or the sandwich is left open in the salon, small amounts of dust and vapours are being ingested.

It is unlikely that this will affect a client as they will drink a coffee or eat a sandwich in the salon so infrequently. A technician, however, could be doing this every day and several times a day. The levels will soon build up.

Simple rules to follow would be:

- Do not drink hot liquids at the desk; it is possible for them to absorb vapours from the air
- Avoid placing any drinks on the desk, as the container could collect dust
- It is possible for uncovered food to absorb vapours; keep all food away from the salon
- Wash your hands before eating anything, even a small bit of chocolate.

Absorption

Every time a chemical, even water, touches the skin or nails, an amount of it will be absorbed into the skin. The body is quite happy to have thousands of different chemicals enter the upper levels of the skin. Specific cells within the blood maintain total vigilance at investigating anything 'foreign' and most of these 'foreigners' are recognized as being friends and are left alone. However, there will also be many 'foreigners' that are not recognized as friends, and they will be removed and destroyed. These cells will recognize these non-friendly chemicals if they appear again and may just remove and destroy them without any fuss. However, if these foes continue to appear the blood will develop a substance that will fight them and this is when a reaction is noticed.

- The most obvious reaction is irritated skin in the area of absorption. If the irritant is not immediately removed, this can develop into a very painful skin condition that will take a very long time to go.
- Local irritation is not always the first sign of an allergic reaction. Puffy or itchy eyes could be a reaction to a product on the nails. Headaches, tiredness, mood swings, nosebleeds, dizzyness, coughs, or a sore throat can also be signs of a reaction to the chemicals via any of the routes of entry.
- If the irritating chemical is removed the symptoms should also disappear. They will however reappear if the chemical is reintroduced, as once the body is sensitized it will always be sensitized. From the point of view of a technician, if this sensitivity is created to a commonly used product it may be difficult to find an alternative. This could mean that the technician can no longer work, which is a very drastic result of what amounts to laziness or lack of understanding. For a client, it can be very distressing and they may be lost as a client or, worse, take legal action against the salon or technician.

HEALTH AND SAFETY
Don't assume that any new symptons are just tiredness or stress

As these potential problems can all be avoided with a little extra care and a real understanding of the work, it is not worth taking any risks.

Hygiene products

STERILIZATION, DISINFECTION AND SANITIZATION

Hygiene in the salon can be divided into three categories:

- **Sterilization**: this process kills all living organisms and needs to be used on metal tools as they may have come into contact with body fluids.
- **Disinfection**: this will kill some living organisms and inhibit the growth of others and must be used on hard surfaces and tools and equipment that do not come into contact with body fluids.
- **Sanitization**: this will inhibit the growth of certain living organisms and must be used to clean hands and prepare nails for treatment.

We will look at each of these in more detail.

Sterilization

There are only a few items used in the process of applying artificial nails that need to be treated with sterilization methods but they do, however, need careful treatment. It is a legal requirement for salons to have suitable sterilization methods in place and local Environment Health Departments can have differing requirements. Before choosing a system for the salon it is worth checking the local requirements.

The reason for such stringent requirements is that the risk of the spread of disease must be minimized. Body fluids such as blood and lymph could carry viral infections such as hepatitis or HIV.

Tools to be sterilized

The tools that could carry this risk factor that are commonly used are cuticle nippers, nail clippers and cuticle knives – that is, anything with a sharp edge or blade. These are easily sterilized.

Tools that are not so easily sterilized and sometimes carry the same risk are files and buffers. Occasionally, a technician may break the skin with a file or buffer around the nail plate or sometimes clients have such delicate skin at the side of the nail or a hangnail so that rough handling breaks the skin. If this happens the only safe action is to discard any file and buffer that has been used. Wood, paper and sponge are not satisfactorily sterilized.

Sterilization methods

There are many sterilization methods available on the market. A very large salon may benefit from the larger and more costly equipment, such as an *autoclave* which uses extreme heat to destroy bacteria. There are some systems that provide the facility of sealing the tools into a bag that then goes into a unit to sterilize them. The tools are removed from the bag only when needed. As tools are sterile and germ-free until they come into contact with air, this method keeps them as hygienic as possible until required.

Another method that would probably be most suitable for smaller salons would be that of *chemical sterilization*, where the tools are immersed into a solution for a minimum period. Checking with local Environmental Health Departments is recommended for this, as some brands are not recognized in certain areas. Care should be taken when using the chemicals as they are very strong irritants and should never come into contact with skin. The directions should also be carefully followed as they usually need diluting with water and only specific dilutions are effective over certain time periods.

In preparation for all sterilization methods, tools should be scrubbed with a soapy water or a solvent to remove any grease or debris and then carefully dried with disposable towels. This needs to happen before sterilization.

Ideally, all metal tools should be sterilized after every client; however, in the 'real' salon environment, this is rarely practised. If there is any possibility at all of a break in the skin or contact with a skin or nail condition, the process must be rigorously followed. If this is not the case and the skin and nails are healthy, then metal tools can be wiped with a solvent to remove grease and debris and immersed in a **disinfectant** solution for the recommended time.

HEALTH AND SAFETY
The smallest nick or cut on anyone's hand should strigger a complete sterilization procedure

Disinfection

Work surfaces

There are many areas that require regular disinfection. This process will destroy many bacteria, viruses and fungal spores and is essential for general salon hygiene.

All hard surfaces should be cleaned on a regular basis with a disinfectant solution. For example, desks should be wiped over after every client, preferably with a weak disinfectant; they should have a thorough clean at the end of every day. Floors, light switches, sinks and basins should all be cleaned with a disinfectant on a regular basis.

Towels

Terry towels used during treatments and those used to dry hands should be washed with the addition of a suitable disinfectant solution. Commercial disinfectants are often available at beauty wholesalers or cleaning-product wholesalers that are suitable for all these jobs. Some beauty and nail product companies also supply products designed for this use.

Tools

All tools need some form of disinfectant and there are branded products available for this together with suitable equipment to carry out the process easily and efficiently. *All* reusable tools must be disinfected after every use and, like the sterilization solutions, the manufacturer's instructions should be followed carefully. The only acceptable exceptions to this rule are brushes used to apply acrylic overlays. Disinfecting these brushes would destroy them; they are used with solvents so are unlikely to be a health risk, and they do not touch any soft tissue (see separate instructions for cleaning).

Files and buffers

Files and buffers used in any treatment should either be disposable, personal to specific clients only, or be of a quality that can be submersed in water.

A recommendation for every nail desk would be to have a disinfectant solution in a suitable container where all metal tools are stored waiting to be used. When they are needed, they are removed and dried with a paper towel. When they are finished with and do not need sterilizing, they should be wiped with a solvent and returned to the disinfectant, care being taken not to remove them before the recommended time period (usually around 15 minutes).

Used files and buffers should be stored in a covered container until they can be cleaned of dust and then placed in the disinfecting solution. After the minimum time period, they can be removed, rinsed to remove the solution and left on paper towels to dry.

Sanitization

This is a process that is essential for the cleansing of hands and the preparation of nails. Skin cannot be sterilized or disinfected as the chemicals that can do this are irritants and sometimes corrosive. Sanitization is the lowest level of **decontamination**, but is necessary to avoid the spread of diseases and, in the case of nail preparation, is essential to maintain healthy nails.

Technicians

Technicians' hands should be washed before and after every treatment for the safety of themselves and their clients. It not only limits the spread of bacteria and viruses, it also removes traces of artificial nail products and dust.

Washing hands in soap and water is not always enough. Ideally, an antibacterial soap should be used that has moisturizers to prevent the skin becoming dry. Hands should be dried with paper towels as terry towels can become an efficient breeding ground for bacteria and there is some proof that hot air driers can also cause problems with bacteria.

Clients

Clients should also have clean hands but nails are 10 times more absorbent that skin. Once a client has washed their hands with soap and water it is possible that the nails have absorbed quantities of water and the soap used could have left traces on the nail plate. If washing with water is preferred by the salon and client, ask the client to avoid the area of nails.

There is another alternative which has many advantages over soap and water. There are many *hand sanitizers* available on the market which have the ability to cleanse skin more efficiently without the use of water or drying the skin. The advantages are that the technician and client can cleanse their hands at the desk so both can be confident that it has been carried out; a good-quality product will be more efficient that an antibacterial soap and water: there is no water absorbed into the nails that may carry bacteria and will then be trapped there with the application of an overlay. The sanitizer should be applied, liberally, to the hands which are then rubbed together and wiped dry with paper towels to remove any debris. The technician should, however, make a point of washing their hands regularly to avoid any build-up of product.

Nail preparation, dealt with below, also involves sanitization (not sterilization as some people think). It is an essential stage in any treatment and extreme care must be taken to ensure it is done efficiently and correctly. The nail plate under artificial nails can be an incubator for bacteria and fungi, as it is warm and moist. The technician must make absolutely sure that there is no bacteria or fungal spores on the nail plate or that the conditions are right for their growth.

LEGISLATION FOR SALONS AND EQUIPMENT

There are many Acts and other pieces of local legislation that refer to salons with five or more employees; however, much of it is common sense and it is advisable that all technicians make themselves aware of these regulations.

All necessary information and ready-made forms are available in the HABIA *Health & Safety Implementation Pack.*

Control of Substances Hazardous to Health (COSHH) Regulations (1994)

This provides the requirements that control exposure to potentially hazardous substances. As many nail products fall into this category, this is a very relevant Act for technicians. It is relevant to employers, who must identify the potentially hazardous substances, assess their risk to the salon and staff and provide the measures that need to be taken to minimize risk or control exposure and ensure that staff are fully informed. This is recorded on a *Risk Assessment* form (see example). The recorded information is relevant only if there are five or more employees but, owing to the nature of the products, it is a very good idea to carry out these requirements for even a single technician. Some insurers require this documentation regardless of the size of the salon.

All products should have a **Material Safety Data Sheet** (or MSDS) available from the manufacturers or distributors. These do not always accompany products when they are purchased but, without them, the legal requirements of this regulation cannot be

HEALTH AND SAFETY
Read and learn the COSHH Regulations as they affect your work

HEALTH & SAFETY – RISK ASSESSMENT

Compiled by:			Date:		Review Dates:		
Action Point	Hazard	What is the risk/ who is at risk?	Degree of risk High/Med/ Low	Action to be taken to reduce/ control risk	Staff Member Responsible	Completion Date	
						Target	Actual
9a	No first aid kit	Everyone in the salon	High	Obtain first aid kit and appoint person to take charge of first aid	Julie, Salon Manager	2/11/98	

We have allocated each Act or Regulation a number. Each point in the Act has a letter. 9a refers to Regulation 9, point a.

EXAMPLE

Copyright © 1999 Hairdressing Training Board Limited   HSIP 1

carried out. If a relevant sheet is not provided automatically, contact the manufacturer or distributor and ask for a copy. Collect copies of the MSDS for every product that is stocked and keep them in a file that is readily available, together with the Risk Assessments. An MSDS provides the information on things such as how to store the product, what are the specific **hazardous ingredients**, emergency first aid advice, possible routes of entry, how to deal with large spills and similar advice.

Many of the products in use in the nail industry are manufactured in the US and the requirements for their MSDS differ from those required in Europe. They tend to be a bit more complicated, but the required information is there. A technician should make sure from the supplier that the MSDS is completely compliant with EU regulations.

Health & Safety at Work Act (1974)

Again this relates to an employer, but many of the requirements make good sense for everyone to follow.

The Act requires that:

- all equipment is safe
- all products are stored and handled safely
- the workplace is a safe place to be with regard to fire, first aid and the recording of accidents
- the employer has ensured that all staff have been trained and are aware of all the relevant safety issues – for example, where firefighting equipment is kept and which type of equipment is appropriate for various types of fire.

HEALTH AND SAFETY
Do you know where the fire extinguisher is kept and how to get out in the event of a fire?

The Electricity at Work Regulations (1989)

Where any electrical equipment is used, such as a UV lamp or desk lamp, there are certain rules to follow. Failure to do this could have implications for insurance policies and local authority licensing.

The Act requires that:

- the electrical supply is regularly tested by an approved electrician
- all the electrical equipment is listed on a salon register
- all equipment is regularly tested and the test recorded
- all staff are able to recognize any visual fault and are competent in the use of the equipment.

The Health & Safety (First Aid) Regulations (1981)

Again this relates to employers and refers to the availability of a first aid kit. However, owing to the nature of the work, every technician should have access to a suitable first aid box. Suitable kits are available from High Street chemists and beauty wholesalers.

HEALTH AND SAFETY
Do you know where the first aid box is kept?

HEALTH AND SAFETY FOR HAIRDRESSERS

ROUTINE HEALTH & SAFETY INSPECTIONS

Salon Name:

Inspection Items/Areas	Staff Member Responsible	Inspection Dates/Initials			
HOUSEKEEPING	Jane Jones	6/1/99 JJ	8/2/99 JJ		
FIRST-AID KIT	Tanya Brown	6/1/99 TB	2/2/99 TB		
ACCIDENT BOOK	Tanya Brown	6/1/99 TB	2/2/99 TB		
FIRE EXITS/ EXTINGUISHERS	Damion Giles	10/1/99 DG	4/2/99 DG		
FIRE DRILLS	Damion Giles	10/1/99 DG	4/2/99 DG		
GENERAL HEALTH & SAFETY INSPECTIONS	Marion Page	2/1/99 MP	1/2/99 MP		

EXAMPLE

Copyright © 1999 Hairdressing Training Board Limited   HSIP 5

ELECTRICAL EQUIPMENT REGISTER

Salon Name:				
No.	DESCRIPTION	SERIAL NUMBER	DATE OF PURCHASE	DATE OF DISPOSAL
1	Black Turbo Hairdryer	SN002756733	20/1/91	26/2/98
2	Cash Register	XXM-666743A	2/3/93	
3	Microwave	ZNA0098235561	3/9/97	
4				
5				
6		**EXAMPLE**		
7				
8				
9				
10				

Copyright © 1999 Hairdressing Training Board Limited   HSIP 7

HEALTH AND SAFETY FOR HAIRDRESSERS

ELECTRICAL TEST RECORDS

Salon Name:

Names and Addresses	Phone Number	TARGET	ACTUAL	TARGET	ACTUAL	TARGET	ACTUAL
ELECTRICAL CONTRACTOR Goldman Bros. 22 Cantley Terrace Smithton GG7 1FY	324-6690	4/3/98	10/3/98	4/9/98	22/10/98	4/3/99	
		EXAMPLE					

HSIP 6

ACCIDENT BOOK

Salon Name:

When did the accident happen? *Give date and time*	Where did the accident happen?	How did the accident happen? *Give as much detail as possible*	Who was involved in the accident and what were the injuries (if any)?	Who investigated and recorded the details in this book? *Give full name and position*	Was the accident reportable under RIDDOR?

Copyright © 1999 Hairdressing Training Board Limited   HSIP 10

FIRE EQUIPMENT TEST RECORDS

Salon Name:		TEST DATES					
Names and Addresses	Phone Number	TARGET	ACTUAL	TARGET	ACTUAL	TARGET	ACTUAL
FIRE EQUIPMENT CONTRACTOR Sampson Fire Sampson House Wellington Lane Smithton GG2 2HH	324-1681	4/3/98	10/3/98	4/9/98	22/10/98	4/3/99	
		EXAMPLE					

HSIP 11

The Reporting of Injuries, Diseases and Dangerous Occurrences Regulations (1995)

This is a very important piece of legislation and applies to all technicians – employed, employers, salon-based, home-based or mobile. The Act requires that:

- very serious accidents are reported to the Environmental Health Officer (EHO) immediately
- serious accidents are recorded and the EHO is informed within 10 days
- all other accidents or incidents are recorded in an 'Accident Book'.

This applies to both technicians and their clients (see copy of form on page 68).

Fire Precautions Act (1971)

This act provides for the protection of persons from fire risks. Any premises which is designated (this includes any buildings to which the public have access and use as a place of work), requires a fire certificate from the fire authority. This certificate details the use of the premises together with the means of warning and escape in the event of a fire and the means with which to fight the fire. Fire certificates may impose restrictions or requirements that must be adhered to.

The Health & Safety Executive (HSE) have many leaflets that help to make all these regulations easy to understand. These can be obtained from HSE Books, PO Box 1999, Sudbury, Suffolk, CO10 6FS, and some may be available from local Environmental Health Departments.

SUMMARY

The chapter has demonstrated how a safe and comfortable environment may be created and maintained by the technician to comply with all local and national legislative provisions on workplace health and safety.

Preparing You and Your Client

INTRODUCTION

As discussed in Chapter 4, the preparation of the working area is very important for the comfort and safety of both the technician and their clients. There are legal requirements that make sure that working environments are safe places for all. From a technician's point of view, it is important that every client is safe, but clients are in the environment for only a short period of time; technicians are exposed to many hazards during all their working hours, and this chapter builds on Chapter 4 to detail how correct client preparation can be a crucial factor in workplace hygiene and sanitization.

'MAKING A REMEDY INTO A POISON'

There are two quotations from a very useful textbook that are relevant to this issue and are always worth remembering:

- 'The Overexposure Principle'. This rule says, 'Every chemical substance has a safe and unsafe level of exposure. Simply touching, inhaling or smelling a potentially hazardous substance can't harm you. Exceeding the safe level of exposure is the danger you must learn to avoid.'
- 'Paracelus, a famous 14th-century physician, was the first to study and understand toxic substances. He said, "All substances are poisons; there is none which is not a poison. Only the right dose differentiates a poison from a remedy." Over the last 500 years, the public has forgotten what Paracelus discovered. The Overexposure Principle is the modern day interpretation of what he learned.' (Douglas D. Schoon, *Nail Structure and Product Chemistry*, Milady)

Paracelus is correct; everything is potentially a poison, therefore we must avoid the dose that makes the remedy into a poison. It is obvious that the chemicals that are considered a potential hazard on any MSDS, or those that require a warning on their labels, are more likely to have a much lower 'poison' dose than any others. But technicians are not in the position to know what the 'poison' dose for each individual is for each of the chemicals. It is therefore far safer to assume that any dose is a potential 'poison' dose and prevent any problems.

Following all the simple rules for safety in Chapter 4 will ensure maximum protection. Further protection will be gained by following the correct working practices, as described in this book, and also following the manufacturer's instructions as to the use of the various products.

ALLERGIES AND OVEREXPOSURE

There are a couple of frequent queries or worries that keep being expressed by both experienced and new nail technicians. One of them concerns allergic reactions and the other is health and safety in the salon. There are some general rules that should be followed.

Allergies

Allergic reactions and sensitivities can occur to anyone at any time. Unfortunately, this is a very common problem in an industry that handles a variety of chemicals daily. However, it need not be such a problem if good working practices are adhered to, such as practising strict hygiene and not letting artificial nail products touch any soft tissue.

- Any individual, at any time, can become allergic to a particular product or food. It may be something that has been used for years or a few days but there is usually a warning that an allergy has developed, e.g. itchy skin, rash, headaches, etc. This happens when an individual has been exposed to too much of the product but every person's level of 'overexposure' is different.
- If a technician or client develops an unusual symptom, the most common one being an itchy rash on the hands or fingers, there is a likelihood that an allergy is starting. In the case of a technician, they must stop using the product or start wearing gloves and, for a client, to remove all the products immediately. Do not wait to see if it gets worse: it will!
- If these alternative actions are taken quickly enough, the symptoms may go fairly rapidly. If not, the condition will worsen and the hands could become swollen and bleed and the nail plate lifted and distorted. Obviously, the chance of infection at this stage is very high and will make the whole condition even worse. It is really not worth taking the chance of reaching this stage.
- Once the product has been removed, the condition may go. If the client is willing, a different system could be tried which may be successful. If the initial reaction is severe, it would be a good idea to do a patch test in the same way as lash tinting is done. There are a few products that are the most likely culprits in any system. Top of the list is liquid monomer in any acrylic system (or unreacted monomer that may be found as a sticky layer in a UV cured system); an acid-based primer is corrosive so could be the culprit if it has touched the skin;

or sometimes it could be the nail adhesive. It is unlikely that the dust from a cured acrylic will have any effect nor will the dust from a light-cured material as long as there is no trace of the 'sticky layer'. (Excess dust, however, can cause other problems so it should not be considered as safe.)

- If the condition does not go within a few days or if it should seem worse after the removal of all products, the client or technician should get medical advice. It is important to remember that technicians are not medically qualified and should never diagnose any condition. Instant removal of products immediately any reaction is noticed is the only safe course of action, leaving it to see if it gets better is unacceptable.
- There is little point in blaming the manufacturer or seeking recourse if things go wrong. Correct labelling should show all necessary warnings and a professional technician should be aware of how to use all products correctly and safely. We all know household bleach is corrosive and will burn skin and bleach clothes; whose fault is it when this happens with correctly labelled bottles?

'Safe' levels of exposure

A little story that should raise a smile: it is not always easy to explain to some people about safe levels of exposure and how everyone is different. Some just cannot grasp such intangible concepts. A comment I heard recently, from a trainer running a course for beginners learning acrylic who, struggling to explain this to one particular blank face, used an analogy of how products with peanuts seem to have been in the news in recent years as some people have developed an allergy to them. The light suddenly came on behind the eyes and a delighted voice said: 'Oh right, I see now. So which of these products have peanuts in them?'

TREATABLE CONDITIONS AND UNTREATABLE CONDITIONS

As nail specialists, it is important to be able to recognize various nail and skin conditions. There are many common conditions that do not prevent manicures or application of artificial nails, others which need special care and, less commonly, those which prevent any treatment altogether.

Two key rules

Always remember the two key rules:

- Professional technicians are not doctors or dermatologists and therefore should not diagnose a medical condition.
- If there is any doubt about a condition, *do not* continue, but refer the client to a specialist.

It is worth pointing out that if a client has an obvious medical condition of the skin or nails and is treated by a technician without an agreement from their GP or specialist, the technician's insurance can be void and he or she would be directly responsible for any claim against them should problems arise.

HEALTH AND SAFETY
You are not a doctor, so don't diagnose!

Treatable conditions

These are conditions of the hands or nails that do not prevent treatment but understanding of the condition is important as suitable care needs to be taken.

1 **Leukonychia**: white spots on the nail plate. Some people are more prone to these than others and sometimes it depends on the client's job. If white spots are prevalent on most nails, it may be a systemic cause but, more commonly they are caused by minor trauma injuries to the nail plate such as knocking. The spot is where the nail plate layers have separated in a small area. The spot will grow out but is likely to be a slight problem when it reaches the end of the nail, as it may peel.

2 **Splinter haemorrhage**: tiny black streaks under the nail. Usually due to minor trauma and occasionally due to illness. They will grow out.

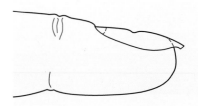

Splinter haemorrhage

3 **Beau's lines**: horizontal ridges across the nail plate. Mechanical trauma, e.g. overbuffing of artificial nails or systemic causes, for example, illness, drugs, skin disorders around the cutical area. They will grow out.

4 **Lamellar dystrophy**: peeling or flaking nails. Usually caused by dryness. Use gentle filing with a very fine emery board, moisturize nails and cuticles and avoid too much water, detergents, etc.

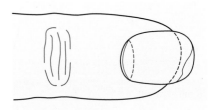

Beau's lines

5 **Onychophagy**: nail biting. Frequent manicures will help stop this problem as the cuticle can be treated immediately to improve appearance and condition which is often enough encouragement to stop the habit. Artificial nails can be applied but must be kept very short (to the end of the finger) and the client must return weekly until the natural nail has grown enough to support the artificial one.

6 **Furrows**: longitudinal lines from matrix to free edge. A single furrow may be congenital or caused by injury to the matrix. Multiple furrows are usually caused systemically. Treat with care as the furrow may be very thin. Do not overbuff to try to smooth the ridge as this will cause splitting.

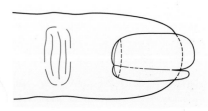

Lamellar dystrophy

7 **Onychorrhexis**: longitudinal splitting associated with furrows. As above but thinned nail splitting along ridge. Treat with great care as the nail is delicate. If there is no inflammation or infection, an overlay could be applied to repair the split and prevent further splitting. As the fault is in the matrix, the condition is usually permanent. Strong, healthy nails can be encouraged by careful treatment that will help avoid splitting or a permanent overlay will solve the symptom, not the cause.

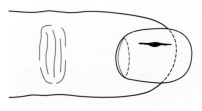

Onychorrhexis

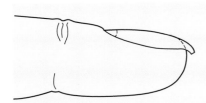

Eggshell nails

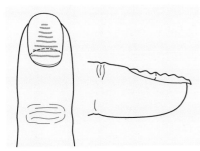

Habit tic

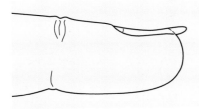

Koilonychia

8 Blue nails: nails with a bluish tinge. Usually poor circulation. May be illness. Nails are often weak and thin. Hand massage and careful buffing will stimulate the circulation in the area. Artificial nails are not recommended if the nails are very thin as the treatment will cause too much trauma to the nail.

9 Hangnail: small tear in the cuticle or sharp point on side of the nail. Neglect of cuticles or dryness. The nail fold, if neglected, will often stick to the nail plate and, as the nail grows, is pulled with it. If this happens and the skin is overstretched, it will split at the sides leaving a ragged corner. The lateral folds (side walls) can often produce sharp points of skin. Both of these may be carefully removed with a clean pair of nippers. This condition can be prevented by gently lifting the nail fold, when softened, from the nail bed and keeping it moisturized.

10 Bruised nails: dark spots of blood under the nail plate. Avoid the area if painful, if there is pressure under the nail or the bruise covers more than a quarter of the nail. Otherwise treat gently. The blood will eventually grow out.

11 Eggshell nails: thin, pale and fragile nails, usually curving under. Often a sign of chronic illness. Treat very gently.

12 Habit tic: a series of horizontal ridges down the centre of the nail. Caused by picking at the nail fold. Usually associated with a very large and exposed lunula. Advise the client of the damage being done but do not try to buff out.

13 Koilonychia: flat or spoon-shaped nails, thin and soft. Can be caused by iron deficiency or excessive exposure to oils or soaps. Treat gently.

14 Pitting: small pits over the surface of the nail. Usually **psoriasis** or dermatitis. Can be caused by applying a cortisone cream to another area of the body. Treat gently.

Untreatable conditions

These are conditions where the technician must not give any treatment. If you are unsure if you may treat, then refer your client to their GP for permission.

1 Infections/inflammation: if there is any infection or inflammation noticeable, any treatment should be avoided. Not only is there the possibility of aggravating the condition, there is also, in the case of infection, a risk of becoming infected. Examples of this are:
- Infected hangnail.
- **Whitlow** – localized painful, swollen area at the side or base of nail plate.
- **Paronychia** – inflammation of the soft tissue surrounding the nail. Also infectious.
- **Warts** – raised lumps of horny tissue. A contagious viral infection.

2 Onychocryptosis: ingrown nail. More often seen on toes but can be on fingers. Sometimes associated with inflammation and pain.

3 **Onycholysis**: separation of the nail plate from nail bed. Seen as a white area. This can be an allergic reaction and is often associated with a fungal or bacterial infection. If a narrow white area is noticed on several nails, it is usually the beginning of an allergic reaction. All products, including nail varnish must be removed from the nails. If the condition does not improve quickly, the client should see their GP. If the seal is broken under the free edge, fungal or bacterial infections can enter and grow on the nail bed. A GP's or pharmacist's advice should be sought. Sometimes, psoriasis can cause separation but this is usually associated with pitting or other evidence of the disorder.

4 **Onychomadesis**: the nail becomes loose at the cuticle and the new nail pushes old one off. This is usually caused by trauma in the cuticle area. It should not be treated in case infection develops under loose nail.

5 **Onychomycosis**: **lifting**, discoloration or rotting of the nail plate. A fungal or bacterial infection. Some fungi feed on the non-living keratin of the nail, others on living tissue. Any infection must be avoided and the client referred to a GP.

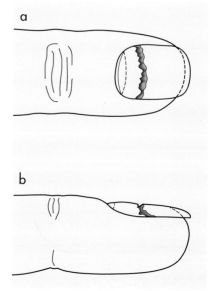

Onychomadesis
a from the top
b from the side

CLIENT CONSULTATION AND ASSESSMENT

Initial information

Assessing the client for treatment is a very important part of every client's appointment. It is a requirement in the National Occupational Standard and the keeping of records is a requirement for insurance purposes. It is widely accepted that the first appointment with a new client warrants a client consultation; what is very often missed is the importance of a consultation before every treatment. A full client consultation should provide a great deal of important information:

- **Name, address and telephone number**: this is obvious but a very useful tool for the professional technician. The address can provide the facility to do mail shots, send invitations to special events, greetings cards, etc. Record of a daytime and evening telephone number can also be essential if a problem arises with an appointment, such as a technician who is unwell. A timely call to the client can avoid unnecessary travel or upset schedules.

- **Date of birth**: this is a recognized part of an individual's identification but not necessary information for a nail technician. Some clients are not forthcoming with their date of birth and it can be an optional requirement. One use for it would be to send a regular client a birthday card as a good PR exercise. If a technician suspects a client is under 16 years, then the question of age must be asked, as it is necessary for under 16s to have a letter of consent for any treatment from a parent or guardian.

- **Name of GP**: this is another piece of information that could be considered to be intrusive. There are not many circumstances where a technician would need to contact a client's GP. If medical assistance is sought or approval is needed from a GP, it is the responsibility of the client to get it and the technician to keep that approval on record in case of later problems. There are some advanced beauty treatments where a GP's information would be useful but there is no reason that this should apply to nail treatments.

- **Occupation**: a useful piece of information, not only for conversational reasons but also to give an idea of the type of nails a client could cope with. It could also give an idea as to the reason for any nail and skin problems.
- **Medical history**: with nail treatments, it is unnecessary to go into any medical history in any depth. A client may be quite willing to tell their technician all manner of medical details but what, as a technician, can be done with that information? Without medical training, the implications of the many illnesses and conditions cannot be known. There are some that are relevant in a general way and the main questions that should be asked are:
  - **Allergies**. If a client is prone to allergies, there is a good chance that they may be allergic to some of the products that will be used. If this is the case, it would be a good idea to carry out a skin test or a test nail.
  - **Diabetes**: if a client suffers from this condition great care must be taken with all treatments. Diabetics are slow to heal so any injury sustained during a treatment could result in a problem, and circulation is often poor. Diabetics who do not have their condition under control and are unwell should really have approval from their doctor before embarking on any course of treatment.
  - **Other**: a general enquiry of the client should be made to ascertain if there is any other condition that may be relevant to any nail treatment. Relevant things could be any loss of sensation in the hands or fingers, past nail or skin conditions that may reoccur and heart conditions that may affect circulation in the extremities.
- **Previous nail treatments**: it is worth finding out if the client has received any nail treatments in the past. Results from these treatments would be useful to know as a sensitivity to products may have occurred or the client may be unable to keep artificial nails on owing to lifestyle or habits (like nail biting or picking).
- **The condition of the skin and nails**: this should be noted on the card at this stage. If everything looks healthy and in good condition, it should be noted in case something changes at a later stage. If there is any indication of a skin or nail condition, whether it restricts treatment or not, it must be noted. Obviously any condition that prevents treatment should be noted, together with the recommendations made by the technician. On the occasions when medical approval is necessary the letter should be attached to the card. Sometimes doctors are not prepared to give a letter. If this is the case but

TIP

Be extra careful with clients who are prone to allergies. Avoid skin contact with all nail products and use formaldehyde-free nail varnish.

the client has seen a doctor who has verbally agreed to the treatment, this should be noted on the card and the client sign to say that this is true. The technician has then done everything possible to safeguard both the client and themselves.

If there is any condition, however minor, that is noticed on hands, fingers or nails, it should be noted with a full description. The reason for this is to make sure that the condition does not get worse. Examples of this could be minor nail separation or a minor skin condition on the hands. This is an area where great care must be taken. The technician must be confident that any treatment will be safe. If there is any doubt all treatments should be avoided especially where irritating chemicals are involved.

Treatment advice

The initial information-gathering part of the consultation should provide the technician with lots of preliminary ideas as to potential treatments. This information should be asked in an area of the salon that other clients and technicians cannot overhear, as some people do not want others to know personal details.

The next questions that need to be asked should concern the treatment that the client expects to happen during the appointment. An important piece of information would be to find out exactly *what the client expects from the treatment*. It can often happen that, owing to lack of knowledge or understanding, the client may expect the most amazing results. A common expectation is one where the client thinks that a set of artificial nails will stay on forever and never need any maintenance. Another commonly held belief is that artificial nails damage natural nails. This could mean that the client thinks that they can never have artificial nails as they are not prepared to accept the damage or it could mean that they are ready to accept the damage for the sake of beautiful nails. Obviously this is wrong and the client needs a thorough explanation that damage will not occur if the nails are correctly applied and maintained and homecare advice is followed.

The treatment booked is not always the best one for the client as it may be that another treatment is more appropriate. Reasons for this could be varied but common situations are:

- When the client has reasonably long nails but in poor condition or a bad shape. The client may be unaware that natural nails can be overlayed to strengthen them and correct the shape and has assumed that artificial nails are the only option.
- The client does not realize that a full set of artificial nails requires a commitment of both time and finances. They may be prepared to wait a little longer for long nails and start a course of manicures that still involves time but does not cost as much. If they are not prepared to commit to either the time aspect or the financial aspect it may be better to suggest that they should not have artificial nails as neglecting them will result in damage.

Once this discussion has taken place it is worth reminding the client of all the options available in order that both parties are sure the correct choice is being made. The technician should note down on the record card what the treatment is and what the client's expectations are. This can be referred to later to see if the expectations were fulfilled and it is also useful if another technician treats the client.

Products and aftercare

Details of products used should be noted, if there are options, and some technicians, especially during training, like to make a note of the size of tips used. The importance of aftercare or homecare advice cannot be stressed enough. The easiest way of ensuring this happens is to provide every client with a list of aftercare points with space to add any extra ones. If this list is provided, it should be noted on the record card. Then, if a client returns with a problem and insists that they were not told what to do, it is recorded that this was not the case.

The main points for aftercare are very straightforward and should be adapted to suit product ranges and manufacturers' instructions:

1 Return for all maintenance appointments
2 Do not pick at nails or cuticles
3 If the nails appear to be lifting away from the nail plate, return for repair as soon as possible
4 If any discoloration is noticed, return to technician as soon as possible
5 Do not buff nails in the area of the cuticle as damage can be caused to the natural nail
6 Apply a recommended oil or moisturizer daily to the cuticles
7 Only use a nail varnish remover that is recommended for artificial nails
8 Wear gloves for housework, washing up, etc.
9 Do not use nails as tools
10 Do not do any 'home repairs' to the nails.

All of this information forms the full treatment plan for the individual client and this should be kept in the salon in a secure place. On subsequent appointments, the record card should be available and read through before any treatment begins (see Chapter 9).

CLIENT PREPARATION

After the client consultation has finished, the technician, the client and the nails must be prepared.

Tools and equipment required

- Hand cleanser or antibacterial soap and water
- Cotton wool discs or nail wipes
- Nail dehydrator, sanitizer or acetone

- Clean cuticle knife
- File of 240 **grit** or more.

Cleansing the hands

The first step is to ensure that the hands of both the technician and client are clean and any protective equipment required is in place (such as a mask or a plaster for cuts on the client's or technician's hands).

- The most common form of hand cleaning is using soap and water and preferably an antibacterial soap. If this method is used, great care must be taken to dry the nails and surrounding area. It is better if disposable towels are used for this as this will avoid the spread of any bacteria from unclean terry towels or hot air dryers.
- Ideally, the client should avoid washing the nail area and concentrate more on the hands. The nail plate is many times more absorbent than skin and will retain a small amount of the water and possibly soap. This extra moisture and other chemicals could be trapped in the nail plate and there is a chance that it may cause lifting at a later date. Careful nail plate preparation by the technician should minimize any such problems if the technician is aware of the risk.
- There are many sanitizing gels and sprays available on the market today that can avoid water. These can be used by both the technician and the client at the desk and can often be a much more efficient method of decontaminating the hands. Some branded products will state what bacteria and viruses will be eliminated and many will be much more effective than antibacterial soap and water. There is also the additional benefit of not having to leave the desk.
- Another very important benefit is the avoidance of water. With this method, there is no possibility of excess water being absorbed into the nail plate. There are some manufacturers who recommend that nails should not be overlayed for at least 30 minutes after hand washing with water to give time for the water to evaporate.

HEALTH AND SAFETY Do not begin any treatment on unsanitized hands

Preparing the nail plate

After hand cleansing comes the essential stage of preparing the nail plate. This is often a stage that is not thoroughly understood by technicians or is rushed owing to time constraints. Taking extra care at this stage will save so much time later on and, more importantly, will avoid problems than can occur that could cause damage to the natural nail:

Removing the cuticle

- The **true cuticle** is a thin, clear layer of skin that is attached to the nail plate. It grows continually and there is always some to be removed. It is possible, if a client has not had a manicure or any nail treatment for some time, that the cuticle could be covering the lower part of the nail. As it is so thin and transparent it is difficult to see. Removal of this is essential as any overlay products will not bond to this skin, they will bond only to a clean nail plate. A little area of missed cuticle will cause lifting of the overlay that, in turn, can result in other problems. The nail fold at the base of the nail must never be pushed or forced, especially when it is not softened. It is not recommended to apply any products to soften the nail fold at this stage, as they will be difficult to remove and may be absorbed by the nail plate. If the nail fold is unsightly, the technician should recommend that the client has a few manicures first to minimize the skin.

- Before touching the nail with any tools, wipe each nail over with a sanitizing product that is recommended for this use. In the absence of a suitable product, acetone or a nail dehydrator could be used.
- The correct way to wipe over the nail is to dampen a piece of cotton wool or similar and wipe the surface of the nail from the tip of the finger towards the cuticle area. In this way oils from the skin will not be drawn on to the nail. This will leave the nail plate clean and minimize the risk of contamination.
- Before applying artificial nails, the most efficient method of removing the cuticle is with a clean cuticle knife. There are many to choose from on the market. Some can have a very sharp blade but every metal tool needs to be used carefully as they can cause severe damage to the nail plate.
- This stage must never be missed and the whole nail must be checked for cuticle. With practice, it is often easier to feel the cuticle rather than see it. With so many different cuticle tools available, it is advisable to get advice from the distributor on the correct use.
- As a general guide, hold the cuticle knife reasonably flat on the nail plate and, starting around the centre of the nail, gently scrape down towards the nail fold. Any cuticle on the nail plate will be easily removed if the knife is held at the correct angle and the nail will not be affected. If the knife is held upright it is possible to dig into the nail. Once the whole nail has been checked for cuticle, special attention needs to be paid to the sides of the nail. The skin can be pulled back by a finger and thumb and the cuticle knife can check for cuticle down the side walls.
- The nail fold at the base of the nail should be gently lifted, never forced. An efficient cuticle knife in the correct hands should accomplish this without any problems. The knife should then be used to clean away any debris from around the edges and nail fold.
- A wooden orange stick is not suitable for this job of removing the cuticle. It is good for gently lifting and shaping the nail fold during a manicure but is not able to remove cuticle as efficiently as a good cuticle knife.

Removing the shine

- A nail plate is naturally smooth and fairly shiny. This helps it to resist too much moisture absorption as the surface is, in a way, 'sealed'. Two shiny surfaces do not bond together with an adhesive as efficiently as a rough surface as there is not enough 'grip'. (This could be likened to a shiny leather sole on a new shoe and a smooth pavement. There is no grip, but if the sole is scored to make it rough, it will grip much better.) The adhesive or overlay has more surface to hold onto if the shine has been removed.
- The nail plate, like the skin all over the body, has bacteria living on the surface. Some of this bacteria is harmless and sometimes useful. Other bacteria may not be so friendly so, when applying artificial nails, it is safer to try to remove all the bacteria. Using a gentle abrasive to remove the shine on the nail will also help to remove some of these unwanted 'visitors'.
- The natural nail should never have an abrasive used on it that has less than a grit of 240 as it would cause too much damage. The end of a file of 240 grit or less is ideal to remove the shine. The end shape can get very close to the nail fold without causing damage to the soft tissue, and the sides of the file are perfect for getting down inside the side wall and ensuring there is no area of nail missed. The file should be used in the direction of nail growth, that is from the cuticle area towards the free edge. Keeping this one direction only will minimize any trauma to the nail plate and help to avoid any more of the surface being removed than is necessary. It is literally only the shine that needs removal and not a layer of nail or any amount of nail that will make the nail plate thinner.
- When the entire surface of the nail has been gently filed the free edge, if there is any present, can be tidied up and shaped to fit in to the tip (see Chapter 6). At this stage the nail plate should look dull all over.

Dehydrating the nail plate

- It is essential that the nail plate does not have any trace of oil or moisture on the surface immediately before application of the overlay. Oil or moisture could be carrying bacteria or fungal spores that could cause problems, and any overlay or adhesive will not bond to the nail if there is any oil or moisture present.
- Obviously, the nail bed is excreting natural oils and moisture that keep the nail healthy and flexible and this will continue. This moisture will not affect the overlay once it is bonded to the nail but the bond must occur while the nail plate is moisture-free.
- As the nail plate has a surface that is slightly more porous than usual, owing to the removal of the shine, any dehydrator used on it will penetrate the upper layer very slightly and

TIP

If there is any delay after dehydrating the nails, repeat the process.

remove excess moisture that is present. Dehydrators used on the nail plate not only remove excess moisture but they also act as sanitizers. Most bacteria and fungi require moisture to live, and by removing this essential moisture any organisms that are present will not be able to survive. The mild products used for this purpose will not necessarily kill the organisms, as the products must be mild enough to be used on the skin, but they will stop or inhibit the growth so any organisms will not survive.

- As before, the product designed to be used for this job (or acetone) should be applied following the manufacturer's instructions. Alternatively, the dehydrator can be wiped over the nail on a cotton wool disc or nail wipe towards the finger. This will remove the dust that has been generated by filing.

- The nail is now perfectly clean and prepared and ready for the application of artificial nails. It is at this stage that the client must be prevented from using the prepared hand and the best way to avoid this happening is to ask the client to keep their hand flat on the towel. It is so easy for the client to use this hand to touch their face or head and then all the preparation work is lost as oil, moisture or make up could have been transferred to the nail plate.

- If the nail system that is going to be applied to the nails does not involve a lamp for curing, it is best that each hand is prepared and all artificial nails applied before the next hand is started. In this way the client always has one hand free and there is no chance of contaminating the prepared nails.

  If a system using a lamp is being used, then both hands need to be prepared as while one hand is in the lamp, the other is being worked on. In this case, the client must keep both hands on the desk and the technician must make sure this happens.

THE PROCEDURE OF NAIL PREPARATION

To recap:

1 Wipe over all the nails of one hand with a sanitizer
2 Remove the cuticle and gently lift the nail fold
3 Remove the shine on the nail plate and shape the free edge
4 Dehydrate the nail plate and remove debris
5 Continue to next stage.

SUMMARY

This chapter has explained how correct 'client management' – awareness of treatable and untreatable conditions, safe exposure levels and hygiene/sanitization procedures – can create a safer workplace for both technician and client.

CHAPTER 6

Applying Tips to Nails

INTRODUCTION

There are two methods of lengthening nails: one is by applying a plastic tip to provide the length and then the overlay goes over the top; the other is by 'sculpting' the overlay onto the nail to provide the length (see Chapter 8). This chapter deals with the application of the plastic tips and is relevant to all the different nail systems as it forms the basis of this method of applying artificial nails.

APPLYING A PLASTIC TIP

Plastic tips come in many shapes and sizes, colours and lengths. Some of them are amazing to behold and all of them, to the beginner, look impossible!

Applying the tip is a skill in its own right and one that is often hurried during training in an effort to get on with overlay application. The application of the tip must be perfect and on completing this stage, the nails must look like they actually grew on the finger and are not a piece of plastic stuck to the end. If the tips are not a perfect fit, they cannot be corrected by the overlay. The shape of the overlay has its own rules and requirements, and must not be concerned with correcting a badly applied tip.

The tip plays only a small part in the strength of the finished nail. The most important area of strength is provided by the overlay. The tip alone is only as strong as the bond between it and the natural nail and this is not a good bond. If the real strength is not provided by the overlay, the tip will snap off. A well-applied tip does provide some strength in one area and that is the side wall near to the free edge. This area of nail, either real or artificial is very vulnerable, and is the most usual place for a nail to break. A tip will add some strength here.

Nail with area of tip highlighted to demonstrate reinforcement of vulnerable area

ABS plastic or acetate tips

A good-quality tip is made from 'virgin' ABS plastic. ABS is a plastic within the acrylic family; it is a relatively strong plastic that can be made in many different colours. Most tips today are made from ABS plastic, but occasionally a tip may be made from another type of plastic called acetate. These tips have a translucent quality and are usually more transparent than traditional tips. They tend to be cheaper and were originally made for the false nails that were sold for retail use to be stuck over the whole nail. These are not suitable for artificial nail systems as they are difficult to blend into the natural nail and have a higher oil content that may affect the overlay.

Making the tip

Tips are manufactured by pouring liquid ABS plastic into a mould that is shaped rather like a tree with a central 'stalk' and the tips coming out of the side like branches. The little rough bits on the end of tips show where there were removed from the main 'stalk'. The 'stalks' that are left after the tips have been removed are sometimes used by manufacturers to be melted down and reused to make more tips (rather like remould tyres). This obviously helps manufacturers to keep costs down but, like some remoulded tyres, the tips can have weak spots. 'Virgin' plastic is a plastic that has been freshly made and not mixed with the melted 'stalks'.

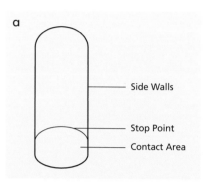

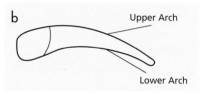

Features of a tip
a the front
b the side
c the end

Important features

Every tip, whatever its shape or size, has a number of features that are relevant to the technician:

1 **Contact area or well**. This is a thinner area that is the part that is in contact with the natural nail.

2 **Stop point**. This is the demarcation of the contact area and the actual tip. The natural nail free edge should fit snugly into this without any gaps to trap dirt and it will protect the edge of the nail and help it from absorbing too much water. When the tip is properly blended this line will produce a natural-looking smile line.

3 **Side walls**. Tips either have parallel or tapered side walls to suit the natural shape. A well-constructed tip will have a reinforced side to the contact area in order to provide maximum strength in this vulnerable area.

4 **Upper arch**. Like natural nails, tips have different upper arches from flat to very curved. Choose the one that fits the natural nail shape or, if the natural upper arch needs correcting, a flatter or more curved tip may be chosen.

5 **Lower arch**. Like nails that have grown naturally, a tip needs to have a lower arch. This is not so obvious if the shape of the finished nail is going to be oval, but the lower arch is still there and is what make the tip look like it has grown from the finger and not stuck on top.

6 **'C' curve**. As with the upper arch, this can vary between types of tip, and the shape of the natural nail should dictate which is most suitable. Unlike the upper arch, it is not advisable to choose a shape that is different from the natural 'C' curve. The tip needs to sit on the nail comfortably without distorting the shape of the tip. If the natural nail is quite flat

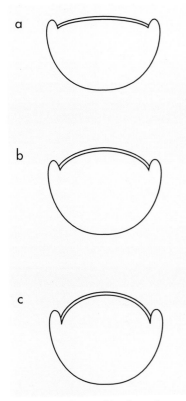

'C' curve of a nail looking from the nail down the length of the finger
a Flat 'C' curve
b Natural 'C' curve
c Deep 'C' curve

and a tip is applied that has a deeper curve, the tip will need to be flattened to adhere across the width of the nail. Once applied, the tip will try to return to its shape and this will put undue stress on the nail bed. When this happens, clients will feel a great deal of discomfort, as the nail bed will throb as if it is bruised. It is even possible that, if the nail plate is very thin, nail separation could occur. If the natural nail has a deep curve and a tip is applied that is flatter, the only way to stick it to the nail is to hold the sides of the tip onto the nail and make it follow the natural curve. Again, after application the tip will try to return to its original shape that may not necessarily cause discomfort but may result in lifting down the side walls.

Choosing the correct tip

Some guidelines

- The first thing to look for in order to choose the correct tip is the 'C' curve of the natural nail. Some nails are quite flat and others are very rounded. This is the starting point in choosing the correct type of tip.
- The next area to take into account is the natural upper arch. If it is flat, it will need some correcting and a tip with a curved upper arch will help. If the nail has a high arch, a curved tip will exaggerate this even more so a flatter tip will help compensate.
- The above are guidelines to help save some time in trying several tips. The best way to choose a tip is to try the tip on the nail. If it follows the curves it is the right one. It is worth a technician having at least two different types of tip available and more if finances allow.

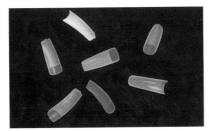
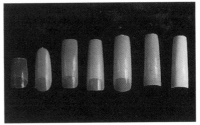

Various types of tips are available on the market. The shape is decided by the shape of the client's natural nail. The design of tip, such as a full contact area or reduced contact area, is a matter of personal preference.

Size and width

- Once the correct tip has been chosen, the right size or width must come next. Most tips come in ten different sizes with 1 being the biggest and 10 the smallest. Sizes 4–6 are the most used.
- When choosing the correct size, the width of the contact area must be ignored and the width at the stop point must be concentrated on. This must be *exactly* the same width as the nail at the smile line (or onychodermal band) without any

gaps when the skin is pulled back from the sides. It is a very common mistake to fit a nail that is too narrow. It cannot always be seen on a new set but when the nail grows, there will be a step at the side with some natural nail exposed. Some clients have puffy or thick skin at the sides of their nails and unless this is firmly pulled back, the full width of the nail will not be seen.

- If one size is too wide and the next is too narrow, choose the wider one and file away a very small amount from either side until it fits perfectly. If there is any doubt as to the correct size, one side of the tip can be 'tucked down' into one side wall and the other side looked at. Very often this will show that a tip that looked right is actually too narrow.
- If a client has a very flat nail and the flattest tip still has the wrong 'C' curve, choose a much wider tip, which will be flatter, and the sides can then be filed until it is the correct width
- **Remember**: always **pretailor** or shape a tip to fit before application as it cannot be changed when it is on the finger.

Reduced contact area

- Some tip types have a reduced contact area. There are several reasons for this. If the tip is an opaque white it is designed to create a quick and easy permanent 'French manicure' look. Although this tip can be used with any system, there are restrictions as to who can wear this tip. The tip must be applied to the end of the nail and not blended. The shape forms a perfect 'smile line' and the overlay will create the necessary strength. This tip is not suitable for:
  1 The client who has a different 'C' curve
  2 A short nail bed, as the extra white tip, when correctly placed, will make the nail look unattractive with too much white and not enough pink
  3 A client without any free edge; the tip's 'smile line' will need to be placed on to the nail bed instead of where it would naturally be and would result in an unattractive nail
  4 A natural nail that does not have an upper or lower arch that matches the tip.
- Other tips with a reduced contact area are a natural colour. These can be used in two ways. Firstly, if none of the above restrictions apply, the tip can be used without any blending as a good overlay will cover the line of the tip. However, if the shape of tip fits the nail, the lack of contact area can speed up blending.

Full contact area

- Most tips have a full contact area. These can be applied directly to the nail plate with adhesive or they can be tailored beforehand. There are eight main reasons why it is worth removing most of the contact area before application:

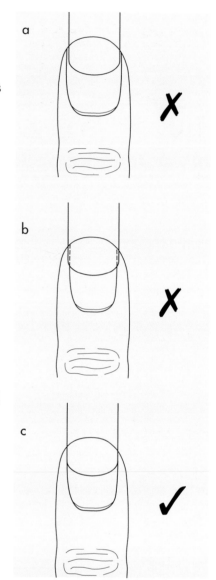

Placing the tip
a Tip too small for nail
b Tip too wide for nail
c Tip of correct size

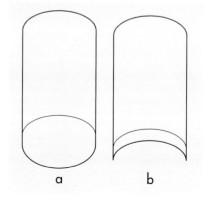

Contact area of tip
a Tip with complete contact area
b Tip with reduced contact area

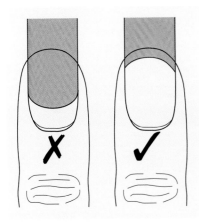

Tip and nail plate
a Tip covering too much of the nail plate
b Maximum nail plate left exposed

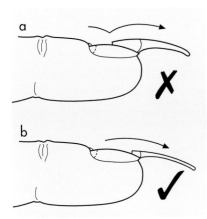

Tip and upper arch
a Tip with complete contact area producing wrong upper arch curve
b Tip with reduced contact area producing correct upper arch

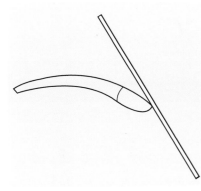

Angle of file to remove contact area

1 When applying a tip with a full contact area it is easy to get bubbles under the tip. If this happens, the tip must be removed. The bubbles are unsightly and could be areas for bacteria or fungus to grow.
2 The bond between the nail and the tip relies on the adhesive used. This will be a cyanoacrylate and this can eventually break down in water. If the bond covers most of the nail there is a larger area to be broken down.
3 The strongest bond in the artificial nail structure is between the nail and the overlay. By leaving most of the nail plate exposed, as in first diagram, the bond will be more effective.
4 A full contact area needs blending until it is invisible and there is no shadow that can be seen through the overlay. This involves more work and there is a greater risk that the natural nail will be buffed. Blending a small area is very quick.
5 When any tip is applied to a nail with a flat upper arch, the contact area must be completely in contact with the nail. A full contact area will cause the tip to be tilted upwards at a very unnatural angle (see second diagram).
6 By having a minimal contact area, the angle of the tip can be placed so that the finished nail looks most natural.
7 By placing the tip at the correct angle with a reduced contact area, the line to be blended will be at the top of the upper arch curve and therefore easier to blend without touching the nail plate.
8 Sometimes the contact area is almost as long or longer than the client's nail plate and there is very little room left to blend the area without damaging the soft tissue. This is particularly the case with nail biters.

Removing the contact area

- There is no rule that states that the contact area must be removed or left in place. However, it is a very useful skill and a thorough understanding of the question allows individual technicians to make up their own mind what is right for their client. The most important result is a natural-looking, strong artificial nail that has been applied without damage to the natural nail and under safe and hygienic conditions.
- There are two methods of removing the contact area:
  1 **Using a file.** By holding the tip and the file at the appropriate angle (see picture) the contact area can be removed very quickly leaving a curved edge. By leaving this shape as opposed to a straight edge, the side walls of the free edge of the natural nail are provided with extra protection and support.
  2 **Using scissors or clippers.** Scissors with a curved blade are ideal for snipping around the contact area following the shape of the stop point. Nail clippers can also be used to cut out a 'V' shape.

Applying the tip to the nail

- Once the tip had been chosen and any necessary tailoring carried out, it must be applied to the nail with adhesive. The choice of adhesive is that of the technician unless the client is a severe nail biter or has a damaged nail plate. If this is the case, a thick adhesive or gel should be used that will fill and cushion the irregularities of the nail plate or, in the case of a nail biter, fill the area where the nail has been bitten down below the hyponychium. If this area is left as an air space, there could be problems with bacteria or excess moisture.

- A small amount of adhesive should be carefully placed in the contact area of the tip. Placing adhesive here is preferable to it being placed directly on the nail. When placed on the nail it can easily run down into the side walls or over the edge of the finger. When placed on the tip it starts affecting the plastic of the tip immediately, softening it ready for accurate placement.

- The tip should be brought to the free edge of the nail at an angle of around 45°. This will allow the nail to be placed correctly in relation to the nail plate and then levered down onto the nail, expelling any air bubbles as the full contact is made. As soon as the excess adhesive is seen being squeezed out onto the nail plate, the tip should be held in place for a few seconds until the bond is made. At this stage, the finger should be pushed up from underneath by the hand that is holding it rather than the tip pushed down. If the tip is pushed down it is very easy to lift it too high and therefore break the contact at the free edge and pull in air.

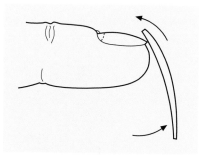

Tip brought to free edge of nail

- This should be repeated for each finger on one hand. When all five tips are applied, they can be cut to slightly longer than the desired finished length. The length should be decided by the client but with advice from the technician if the requirements are unreasonable, such as too long for the nail bed or life style. At this point, it is worth asking the client what shape is required, oval, square, rounded square or tapered. If the client has no preference, the shape of the base of the nail should be followed to create a good-looking nail.

Cutting techniques

- There are several tools available on the market that are designed to make cutting tips easier. They are adaptations of a tool used for clipping animal claws but instead of a round hole that the claw fits through, they have a curved hole for the tip. These clippers are quick and efficient and allow the tip to be shortened with one movement. When using these the metal plate that has the curved hole must be nearer the finger. This will protect the finger from being cut as the blade is on the other side. If the cutter is angled under the client's hand, a slightly curved shape will be cut on the tip. The more upright the cutter is held, the straighter the edge. Care should be taken not to hold the cutter away from the client as

> **TIP**
>
> A good way to practice before applying a tip to a real nail is to take two tips of the same size, put a spot of oil of the top of one tip at the contact area end and 'easing' the second tip on the top of it (as described above) to see how to use the 45° angle to expel any air. The oil can be seen through the tip on top and how it is pushed forward.

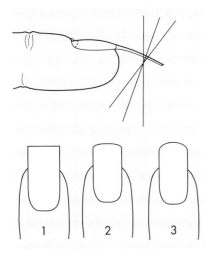

this will result in an edge that curves in the wrong direction and, if the cutter is moved during cutting, could result in pulling the tip off.

- Scissors or nail clippers can be used for cutting tips. Plastic tips are easily 'stressed' or bent which results in white areas. When using clippers or scissors, the tip should never be cut across in one action as this will cause the stress lines. Each side should be cut separately (see picture). The angle of the clipper blade will produce an outline of the finished shape – that is, oval, square or tapered. The piece of tip should be discarded as it cannot be used for anything else.

Angles of one-cut tip cutter
1 = square   2 = rounded square   3 = oval

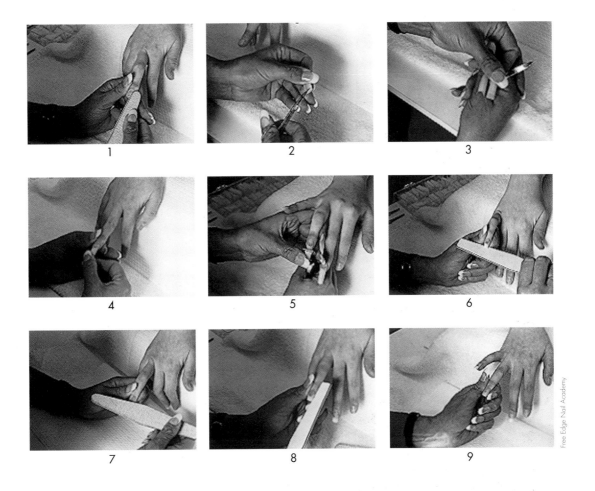

Applying Tips
1 Prepare the natural nail
2 Cut and customize the tip
3 Full well and customized tip
4 Fit the tip

5 Cut tip to desired length
6 File tips to desired shape
7 Blend the seam
8 Slim lateral side walls for optimum elegance
9 Tips fitted and blended

Blending the tip

- Once all tips have been cut to the required length and the unwanted ends discarded, the tips must be blended to the natural nails. The result should be perfectly natural in appearance and look as if a nail had grown there. More importantly, there must be no damage to the nail plate.
- There are two methods of blending the tip: manually – that is with a file – or chemically with acetone or a branded tip blender.

Manual blending

Caution: only a fine grit of 240 or more should be used on the natural nail. Great care must be taken to avoid buffing the nail plate. This is the stage that causes many problems for beginners and removing the contact area of the tip may help.

During training, procedures are easily learned if eight easy steps are followed. These steps will help to produce a perfectly blended tip:

1 Holding the file parallel to the finger, 'tuck' it down in the side walls and, with a few strokes, blend the sides of the contact area of the tip so that it is the same width as the nail plate. By keeping the file parallel, the sides of the free edge will remain straight.

2 Shape the free edge to the approximate shape and length required. Look at the tip on the finger as a whole and not just the nail plate to check that it is a suitable length and shape and it is straight to the finger.

3 Holding the file flat to the tip, gently start buffing the surface, starting at the tip and working backwards towards the contact area. The shine of the tip must be completely removed.

4 Using at least two-thirds of the length of the file, gently buff the contact area. Care must be taken not to buff in the same place for too long. Keep moving the file all over the area but avoiding the nail plate. It is not necessary to press hard with the file as gentle pressure is much more effective. The contact area will become much thinner until it is transparent and cannot be seen. A little nail adhesive often squeezes out onto the nail during the tip application and becomes shiny. This is can be a very useful guide to help know when the tip has been blended and the nail is being avoided. The tip must be completely invisible and there must be no evidence of a 'shadow' where the contact area is.

5 Refine the shape of the free edge until it is perfect and even and remove any debris that may have collected underneath during filing.

6 Look at the nail from the side to check that the upper arch is correct and even and that the lower arch is correct.

7 Gently refine the 'smile line' area to produce a neat and natural-looking effect.

8 The tip should now look like a perfect natural nail and is the ideal 'canvas' to which to apply the overlay.

> **TIP**
>
> A good way of trying out blending before trying it on a real nail is to choose two nails of the same size, imagine one is a 'real nail' and the second is the tip, apply the second tip to the first with adhesive. Using a buffer, blend the tip to the 'nail' as a practice in buffing.

Chemical blending

This method works by melting the plastic of the tip as an alternative to blending with a file. Some people, trainees in particular, like to use this method as they feel that damage to the nail plate can be avoided. To a certain extent this is true, but other problems may occur owing to the nature of the method if it is not fully understood. It is not necessarily quicker than manual blending as, once mastered, manual blending is very fast.

Acetone may be used for this or there are a number of branded products available:

1 Once the tips are applied, paint a small amount of the tip blender with either a disposable cotton bud or a brush used solely for this purpose, over the contact area. Wait a few minutes while the plastic melts. This time can be taken applying the blender to other tips to help speed up the process. Do not apply too much as any liquid can be absorbed into the nail plate and could cause unnecessary dehydration. Too much liquid will also run into the side walls and cause dehydration.
2 While waiting for the blender to work, the free edge can be shaped to the required length.
3 When the tip starts to look very shiny, use a fine file to file away the melted plastic. The blender can be reapplied if necessary but too much solvent on the nail plate should be avoided.
4 The same steps as for manual blending need to be followed now to ensure a perfect nail.
5 Make sure that there is no melted plastic covering the nail plate as this could prevent a good bond with the overlay and could result in lifting in the centre of the nail and an air pocket.
6 Brush the file as the melted plastic can stick to the abrasive and make it less effective. Discard the file if the plastic cannot be removed.

Although skilful manual blending is usually faster, chemical blending is an excellent standby for the client who has very sensitive nail beds and cannot take any buffing on the surface. It is also useful for a nail biter who has such a tiny nail plate that it is difficult to use a file without damaging the soft tissue.

Removing the dust

Once all tips are perfect the dust that has been produced needs to be removed from the nails. A bristle brush may be used but thorough hygiene methods must apply to keep this very clean. Remove dust inside the nail folds with care, making sure that oil from the skin is not brought onto the surface of the nail.

The product being used for preparing the nail plate is often very useful for this job as the moisture will remove the dust and the product will ensure a clean, oil-free nail.

Once the tips are blended and cleaned, they should look like perfect natural nails. If this is not the case and there are shadows of the contact area or the free edge is curving up and not down, they are too wide or too narrow, they cannot be corrected by applying the overlay. No amount of clever overlay application will correct a badly applied tip. It will only make it worse.

PROBLEM NAIL SHAPES AND HOW TO CORRECT THEM

Clients come in all different shapes and sizes, and so do their nails. It is a very lucky technician who gets presented with lots of nails that have beautiful long nail beds with parallel side walls and neat free edges. Most clients present their technician with all manner of horrors and it is the job (and often challenge) of the technician to make the artificial nail look perfect. It is not enough to apply nails that follow the natural shape. Many natural shapes are not perfect and not always very attractive. The technician must correct natural imperfections. Many natural imperfections or problem shapes can start to be corrected with the tip application. This followed by a planned overlay shape will result in the desired perfection.

Practice is the only real way to perfect the art and skill of correcting problem shapes but the following suggestions are a starting point to help that practice along.

Fan-shaped nail

Looking at the nail from the top, the side walls of a good shape should be parallel to each other. A fan-shaped nail is very common and is where the edge of the nail is wider than the base, that is, the side walls 'fan' out. This nail plate is usually quite short and artificial nails can look very wide and clumsy and not at all elegant if the shape is not corrected by the skilful technician.

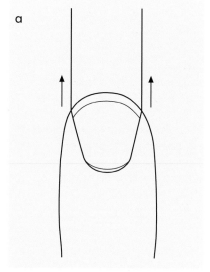

a Fan-shaped nail: fit tip to width at free edge

- The correct tip size should be chosen carefully and the width of the nail plate at the free edge should be the only area to look at to chose the correct size. A tip with a full contact area usually appears much too wide as the contact area will often be wider than the centre of the nail plate. This does not matter as the contact area can be removed. The stop point of the tip must be the exact width of the free edge. Once the correct size is chosen, the contact area can be removed. It is likely that most of the area will need to be removed to avoid it being wider than the nail plate. Sometimes it is also necessary to angle the remaining contact area in so that it fits the nail.
- The tip being tailored should keep being fitted to the nail to make sure the shape is just right. This shape of nail is also usually quite flat with little or no upper arch or 'C' curve. A tip that has a flatter shape should be chosen so as to avoid any stress being put on to the nail bed by a curved nail. If the flatter tip is still too curved to comfortably fit the nail without pressing it flat, a wider tip should be chosen and the sides

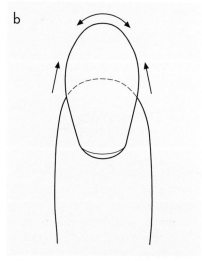

b Fan-shaped nail with blended tip: tapered sides and oval shape

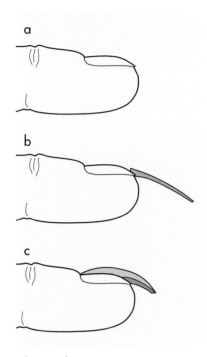

Claw nail
a Claw nail with no free edge
b Tip applied to edge of nail at
  correct angle
c Tip blended and overlay applied
  to correct poor upper arch

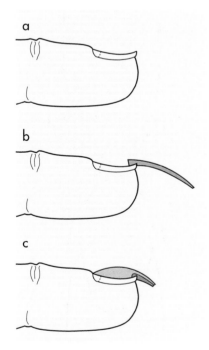

Ski-jump nail
a Ski-jump nail with no free edge
b Tip applied to give better upper
  and lower arch
c Tip blended and overlay applied
  to correct poor upper arch

filed to the correct width. When this has been achieved and the tip has been applied at the correct angle for a gentle upper arch (remembering that the tip will need to be angled down slightly to help create an upper arch), it can be cut to length. It is inadvisable that the free edge is any longer than half the length of the nail bed. Anything longer than this will not look attractive and will not be as strong as a shorter nail.

- When shaping the free edge, the side walls need to be tapered in to compensate for the wide free edge. An oval is often better for this shape of nail as the base of the nail is usually oval, but a square can be achieved if required that does not look too wide. This is achieved by making the parallel side walls taper slightly towards the tip of the free edge. If done correctly, the sides will still look parallel but more elegant than if left, as this can accentuate the 'fan' shape of the natural nail. The square edge can then be achieved. The overlay can then be applied.

Hooked or claw nail

This type of nail has an exaggerated upper arch and the free edge has a tendency to curve over the end of the finger. Clients with this shape nail are often unable to grow their nails as the downward curve is unattractive.

- The solution for this problem is to remove any free edge on the natural nail, choose a tip that fits (this is often one with quite a deep 'C' curve) and remove a great deal of the contact area. When the tip is applied to the nail, the side view should be looked at and the upper arch corrected. Care must be taken that the underside of the tip does not have a gap between it and the nail plate as debris could collect and cause problems.
- The length should be quite short as the longer the free edge, the more the curve will appear. Adjustments in the structure of the overlay will further compensate for this shape.

Ski-jump nail

A relatively common shape, the ski-jump is a nail that curves up towards the tip. If a tip was put onto this shape without any correction, the nails would appear to be pointing upwards.

- The corrective solution is very similar to that of the claw nail. The free edge should be as short as possible and the contact area of the tip removed. As the strength of the finished artificial nail is in the overlay and not the tip, the contact area can be tiny, if necessary, in order to achieve the right upper arch. As before, when applying the tip, look at the side view and make sure the tip is curving down even though the nail bed is curving the other way.
- The length should be quite short and the overlay will need to be adjusted to compensate for the unusual shape produced by tip application.

Bitten nails

Bitten nails are probably the biggest challenge of the technician. If a good-looking set of artificial nails can be achieved from a set of severely bitten 'stubs' the technician can do anything! Obviously there are many degrees of nail biting, from the occasional nibbler to the person who bites their nails down past the hyponychium and on to the nail bed. The worst scenario is the experienced biter who not only bites down onto the nail bed, but also chews and picks at the soft tissue around the nail. The technician can do their best with the nails but can do little, other than offer advice, with the surrounding skin.

- Obviously, recommending a course of manicures before applying artificial nails is preferable as the cuticle and nail fold can be improved and some nail growth will help the strength of artificial nails; however, it is unlikely that the client will agree to this or succeed if they do agree. Biters do not usually bite deliberately and often try to stop the habit. They will try quite hard and achieve a little growth but then, while watching a good film, reading a good book or after a stressful day, will unconsciously nibble and spoil all the hard work. When this happens there is often little point in leaving the other nails so they all go and the biter is back to the beginning.
- Having a set of artificial nails can often be the answer for several reasons. A skilful technician can make the nails and hands look so good the client does not want to spoil them. Having paid for the service the client is more likely to make sure the money is not wasted. The unconscious move to the mouth is immediately noticed as the teeth come across hard plastic instead of soft skin. Nails applied well need determination to bite off, although the biter who is determined will do it whatever it takes!

Preparation

- Although a challenge that will take the technician longer than usual, even the worst biter can have a set of very good-looking nails. The challenge starts with the preparation. A biter will often have a very obvious layer of cuticle and a pronounced nail fold. The cuticle can be removed relatively easily but the nail fold will take more time as it must not be forced. Manicures would help a great deal but this may not be an option. If the nail fold cannot be lifted, it must be left to be dealt with after the artificial nails have been applied either during homecare or manicures.
- The remaining nail plate will be soft owing to the length of time it spends soaked in saliva. There may also be dents and crevices where bacteria can breed. Preparation must be efficient and thorough with the nail and surrounding skin very clean and the nail plate dehydrated as much as possible.
- The skin around a bitten nail is usually puffy, again owing to the amount of time it spends soaked in saliva. The end of the

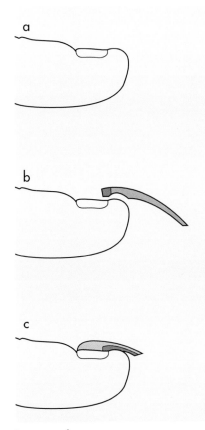

Bitten nail
a Badly bitten nail
b Side walls of tip removed to form
   'bridge' over end of finger;
   contact area also drastically
   reduced
c Tip cut short and blended with
   overlay to compensate for poor
   shape

finger is often slightly swollen from this puffiness, the sides of the nail plate hidden from view and the overall shape flattened. All this will change dramatically after a couple of weeks with artificial nails.

Applying the tips

- Milder cases of nail biting need to have the tips applied in the usual way remembering all the rules about leaving most of the nail plate exposed for the overlay bond and creating good curves. If the nail plate is bitten down past the hyponychium, the skin that is exposed will usually be swollen and higher than the nail plate and the tip will need a great deal of pretailoring before application. A tip, even with the contact area removed, applied to this type of nail will point upwards as the skin will not allow it to lay flat.
- A flat tip needs to be chosen and, if necessary, a wider one made narrow to provide the right 'C' curve (or lack of it). To find the right size the skin at the sides of the nail must be pulled back very firmly with the finger and thumb of the technician so the full width of the nail plate is exposed. Like the 'fan' nail the width at the edge of the nail and the stop point must match exactly regardless of any other part of the tip.
- When the correct size has been chosen (or made) the contact area must be removed so that only a minimal amount of tip will be on the nail plate, leaving the maximum amount of nail plate exposed for the overlay bond.
- At this stage the tip will still not sit on the nail properly as the skin will push it up. The sides of the tip from the stop point down the sides of the free edge need to be carved out for the puffy skin to fit into. This will form a 'bridge' that will curve over the puffy skin and create a reasonable arch that curves down instead of up. This 'bridging' is necessary as without it, not only will the nails look unattractive, the skin that has been pushed down to fit the tip to the nail will be pushing the nail upwards and make it very weak and liable to breakages.
- When applying the tip with adhesive, it is advisable to use a much thicker adhesive than usual. With the skin in the way, the tip cannot be angled onto the nail and needs to be placed from the top. There is also usually an area around where the hyponychium should be that is lower than the nail and the skin. If using thin adhesive, it is difficult to avoid air bubbles when placing the tip in this way and there must not be anywhere that bacteria can thrive. A thicker adhesive will help to avoid the bubbles and fill up and cushion the area of the hyponychium.
- The length must be very short, just to the end of the finger is ideal. The artificial nail will not be as strong as that on an unbitten nail and the client will be unused to having nails and will be clumsy for a few weeks.
- Blending the tip on a small area can be tricky and if it is difficult to avoid the usually delicate soft tissue, it may be

advisable to use a chemical tip blender. Although some people prefer an oval-shaped nail, a free edge that is slightly square usually better suits the wider finger tip of a nail biter.

- The overlay will further improve the appearance of the nails and the homecare advice must be specific, as must the need for maintenance visits.

SUMMARY

This chapter has explored the stages in the process of lengthening a client's nails by plastic tip or overlay techniques – choice, application and safe removal – and how to cope with the many types of 'problem' nails that a client may present to the technician.

CHAPTER 7

Applying Overlays

INTRODUCTION

This chapter explains the differences in all the overlay systems available on the market today. It provides an unbiased information base and explains application techniques with ways to practise and perfect technique.

The perfect foundation has been created with the application of tips. Now is the time to create the perfect artificial nail that looks good and is very durable and strong. The tip has provided the required length, now the **overlay** on that tip will provide the required strength.

'WRAP' TECHNIQUES

By overlaying a tip, a longer artificial nail is going to be created. The overlay can be applied to a natural nail that has some length but needs to be protected as it is weak. Some clients like to wear a natural nail overlay just to keep their nail varnish in perfect condition as it does not chip from an overlay.

This treatment is often known as a '**wrap**'. This term probably came from a technique that was used many years ago by manicurists before the products and techniques we know now were available. If a client had split a nail or had weak nails, a piece of tissue was placed on the nail with a clear varnish. Several coats were applied to smooth the surface. The tissue was sometimes wrapped slightly under the free edge, especially if there was a split. This is where the term 'wrap' came from and is probably the forerunner of the fibre system. Fibre users will now sometimes wrap the fibre mesh under the free edge to seal and strengthen it.

OVERLAY SYSTEMS

This part of artificial nails can sometimes be the most confusing for the beginner. There are several different 'systems' and many different companies, all insisting that their system and brand is the best. Some companies sell all systems, others sell only one of them.

Many clients and technicians believe that the systems look very different from each other. This is often the case, but does not need to be. A beautifully applied set of nails should be a perfect shape and look natural whatever the system. One system need not look thicker or more natural than another. Colours and finishes can make a difference but, the skilful technician can even overcome this with some little tricks of the trade (see Chapter 9)!

The systems in use

Almost all products in artificial nails belong to the acrylic family of chemicals. Acrylics are a vast family of various types of plastic. The word 'system', when it is related to artificial nails, describes the specific method and type of acrylic that produces the overlay.

Each system has a specific collection of various components and it is this collection and the application method that differentiates the systems. The tip application remains the same for each, although various brands may recommend specific preparation products. It is worthwhile taking these recommendations as although cheaper options are often available, specific branded products have been developed to work with the system products to help achieve a better result. Introducing different or additional products or chemicals into the system can lead to problems.

Liquid and powder

- This system is probably more commonly known as 'acrylic', although the term is strictly inaccurate as all the systems are based on acrylics. The system was arguably the first to be used for artificial nails using materials from the dental industry and the term 'acrylic' has stayed since then (see Chapter 1). It uses a liquid monomer and powder polymer (see Chapter 3) that cure to form a solid polymer. Its versatility in the hands of a skilled technician is immense and is generally considered to be the trickiest to learn. It is sensitive to many external conditions, application techniques and the time available to get it right before it hardens is limited. It is, however a very popular system and is the favourite in the UK and US.

- It has many advantages in that any shape can be sculpted on to a tip or a free form (see Chapter 8); it can easily be used to correct difficult nail shapes; powders are available in different colours to allow the technician to create permanent French manicures or enhance the natural skin tones. The overlay can be built to create the strongest structure and the strength within the overlay is excellent.

- Its main drawback is the fact that the monomer is quite volatile and has a strong odour. Many technicians do not like the smell, or the salon may be a beauty salon where strong odours may be inappropriate. This problem can be minimized by working cleanly, correctly and hygienically. There are some products on the market that are classed as '**low odour**'. This usually means that the evaporation rate is lowered. The newer versions of this type of product can work very well and if odours are a problem and a technician prefers a liquid and powder system they are certainly worth considering.

> **TIP**
> This system is considered to be the most skilful. If this is the first one to be mastered, the others will follow with great ease.

- A version of this system that has some additional benefits are the UV **light-cured** liquid and powder systems. These are applied in a very similar way to the traditional acrylics but the main difference is that they do not polymerize until UV light is applied as the catalyst. This can be very beneficial for beginners as they have plenty of time to apply the overlay in the correct shape. For experienced technicians, both hands can be worked on, which avoids any additional time for curing. These monomers are in the 'low-odour' category and therefore can be more user-friendly if odours are a problem. The overlay that is produced is as versatile and strong as traditional acrylic but, with some brands, has a characteristic that must be dealt with carefully. Many UV cured materials do not achieve a total cure and a sticky residue is left on the surface where oxygen has inhibited the cure. This residue is unpolymerized monomer and this is a skin irritant. It must be carefully removed with an appropriate solvent before buffing as continual contact with the skin for either the client or the technician can result in an allergic reaction.
- The liquid and powder systems are applied with a natural hair brush, usually sable or the better quality Kolinsky sable by dipping the tip of the brush first into the liquid monomer and then into the powder polymer where it picks up a bead of the material. This bead is then applied to the nail and pressed into place. Polymerization either occurs within a few minutes or when placed under a UV light if it contains a **photoinitiator**.

UV gel

- The UV gel system could be considered to be a 'pre-mixed' system as there is only one material that is applied. The only other necessity is a UV light source. The gels are available in many different versions, all with different features and benefits. The main differences that will be noticed by a technician immediately is the viscosity (thickness) and how it flows. Some gels are very runny, others are very thick. Some thick gels will eventually flow, others will stay where they are put. Some gels can be coloured, others are clear.
- All gels are applied to the nail and moved around with a brush and then polymerized by placing the nails under a UV light source. As with all systems, there are many application techniques that various companies have developed to suit their gels but there are two basic application methods; one of them is very easy and probably the easiest method of applying overlays out of all the systems; the other is a little more skilful but means that a nail can be sculpted onto a tip for maximum strength.
- Other benefits of this system is that it is virtually odour-free and therefore may be more suitable for use in areas where stronger odours are objectionable. The gels can be very flexible and therefore move more with the natural nail.

- Disadvantages of the system are that some gels and their application methods cannot produce an overlay that is as strong as the liquid and powder systems and are therefore suitable only for those clients who are not too hard on their nails. Many of the gels on the market can be removed only by buffing and not by soaking off with a remover. Some consider this to be a benefit, others consider it to be a disadvantage (see Chapter 9).

Fibre

- The third main system involves the application of a fibre mesh (usually silk or fibreglass) with a cyanoacrylate resin. This is then polymerized or activated with a spray or paint-on chemical. This system is quite a gentle system for the natural nail as the overlay produced cannot be very thick and is quite flexible. It needs very little equipment and the starting costs for trainees is usually relatively low. Odours are kept to a minimum and are negligible if a paint-on activator is used in preference to a spray.
- It is very popular as a natural nail wrap as it is quick and fairly easy and never produces thick, clumsy-looking nails. For manicurists, it is ideal to have to hand as a natural nail repair. The overlay is easy to remove.
- Disadvantages are the fact that the overlay cannot be built up to create a maximum-strength structure and imperfect natural nail shapes can be corrected only by tip application, not a combination of tip application and overlay. As the overlay is quite thin, the artificial nails are not as strong as a structured nail in other systems. Some technicians find the application techniques a bit too 'fiddly' but others love it.

Choosing a system

All the systems have their benefits and disadvantages: it is the technician who makes the difference. Some will hate a specific system and think it does not work at all; another technician will love that system and produce wonderful results. When, as a beginner, the choice of system is a problem and all the marketing and advertising make the choice even more confusing, the best way to choose the right system to learn with is to try them all.

Learning a new skill is so much easier when the task is enjoyable. Learning will take a lot longer and be so much more frustrating if the tasks are unpleasant. Trainees are nearly always under the impression that applying artificial nails is really easy. It looks so easy when an experienced technician does it. It is another story when the trainee tries to do the same and discovers it is not quite like that. As the whole process looks like a 'walkover' it is not enough to watch the various systems being applied. The best way to help decide is to try the options practically to get the feel of how easy (or not) each system may be for you.

A liquid and powder system is not ideal for the person who immediately cannot stand the smell: a UV gel is to be avoided if the 'stickiness' is annoying; fibre should be left alone if handling the fibre suddenly produces clumsy fingers. None of them is immediately easy but, hopefully, one will stand out as being the one that may become easier quicker.

An ideal situation for beginners is to choose a system to learn with, and stay with that system until all the various skills are mastered. At this time, when the technician is very confident in their work, another system can be added. Whatever the system may be it will be very easy to learn as the outcome will always be the same: a beautiful set of artificial nails.

THE STRUCTURE OF THE OVERLAY

The three zones

When applying an overlay, it will help to think of the nail with its tip as having three different **zones**:

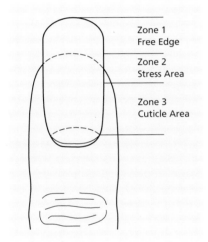

Zones of the nail

- **Zone 1** is the free edge where the overlay needs to be thin on the edge so that the finished nail does not look artificial.
- **Zone 2** is the area over the 'smile line' and slightly on to the nail bed where maximum strength is needed as this is the area of the nail that receives the most stress. It is often called the 'stress area' and should have a highest point that is called the 'apex'. The strongest natural structure is a curve (pressure is dispersed along the curve and is not concentrated over one point). The apex should be where two curves, the upper arch and the 'C' curve, come together at their highest and thickest part. This will create maximum strength for the whole nail without putting any stress on the natural nail, the nail bed, or the matrix.
- **Zone 3** is the last area that is near the base of the nail. Like Zone 1, this should be thin so that ridges on the nail bed are avoided and, by being thin, will be more flexible and able to move with the softer natural nail in this part of the nail plate.

If these zones are always kept in mind when applying an overlay, the correct shape and strength will be easier to achieve.

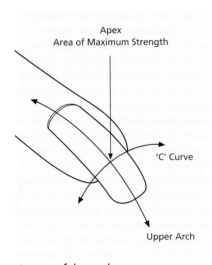

Curves of the nail

The application procedure

The steps in the application procedures listed below are general and, although they will be appropriate for many brands of products, it is advisable checking with the manufacturer or distributor what their recommendations for application techniques are. Always follow manufacturer's instructions when using nail products and always avoid mixing system products from different brands. Polymerization chemistry is carefully balanced and mixing potentially hazardous chemicals could be dangerous and could cause problems.

Liquid and powder

Practising product control: Picking up the product with a brush in such a way that it can be applied to a nail is one of those things that looks so easy. It does, however, take a little bit of practise! For a beginner, picking up the perfect 'bead' can sometimes seem impossible.

- Some liquid and powder brands need a *specific ratio* (this is the amount of liquid to powder), others are less sensitive. There are some brands whose manufacturers recommend that a dry ratio is used in Zone 1 (more powder means harder), a medium ratio in Zone 2 (combination of **hardness** and flexibility) and a wet ratio in Zone 3 (maximum flexibility over softer part of nail).
- Usually the bead that needs to form on the tip of the brush needs to look smooth and glassy.

Practising product control for a little while is time well spent for a beginner. Understanding how the product behaves and practising picking up various beads will save a great deal of time if these first attempts are placed on a nail and either have to be removed or buffed into shape.

- To do this, get a piece of unwanted plastic or glass, dappen dishes with monomer and powder, (use coloured powder as well as clear or pink as they behave differently owing to the density of pigment), a brush and disposable towels.
- Dip the tip of the brush into the liquid and wipe it on the sides of the dish, dip the tip of the brush into the surface of the powder (not deep), hold it there for about 2 seconds and lift it out. It should have a bead of wet product on the tip.
- If the bead is so wet it falls off, there was probably too much liquid still in the brush so it would need to be wiped on the side of the dish a bit more. It may be that the brush needed to be in the powder a bit longer to pick up a bigger bead.
- If the bead that is picked up is rough with obvious powder on the surface, the ratio is much too dry. Maybe there was not enough liquid in the brush or the brush was left in the powder too long and picked up too much powder.

Practise this a few more times until a bead can be picked up that is smooth and glassy in appearance and does not fall off the brush. Different methods of dipping the brush into the liquid can be tried, such as sliding the brush down the side of the dish, noticing how far the brush goes into the liquid, squeezing both sides of the brush on the sides. As a sable hair brush is a natural hair and many brushes are handmade, each one is going to have its own characteristics. One brush may hold much more liquid than another.

Picking up powder: There are also different methods of picking up powder: little circles can be drawn in the surface of the powder or the brush can be drawn through in a line. The brush should never be dipped in further than the tip and there should be sufficient powder in the dish to avoid the brush touching the bottom. If this happens the bead sticks to the dish and is difficult to get out. It is also worth tapping the dish on the desk to smooth out the surface of the powder. A smooth surface makes picking up a bead much easier than one with dips and troughs in it.

Bead control: When a bead can be picked up without disasters, it is worth moving on to 'bead control'. This will demonstrate what the ratio of the bead is and the trainee technician can determine if this is correct.

- This is done by picking up a bead and gently placing it on the plastic or glass. If the bead is on the very tip of the brush it should come off the brush onto the surface with ease. When the bead is on the surface, it should start to melt. How it does this demonstrates if the ratio is correct. By melting, the bead loses its shape and eventually becomes flat.
- All brands are slightly different but, as a general guideline, if the bead melts in less than 3 seconds it has a wet ratio, if it takes over 5 seconds, it is dry. A medium ratio, which is usually the one to aim for, should hold its shape momentarily and then start a slow melt.
- Doing this a few times using the various ways to pick up a bead will show the trainee how to pick up a bead of the right ratio.

This can now be taken a step further. Nails are different sizes and so are the zones on each nail. Now the right ratio can be achieved, it is time to practise picking up a bead that is not only the right ratio but also the right size! A step further again: the right ratio of the right size in a different colour, for example white tip powder. Coloured powder usually needs more liquid owing to the colour pigments present, so this should be tried out first to get the right ratio.

After that, different-sized beads can be picked up to see how much liquid is needed in the brush, how long the brush should be kept in the powder, and so on. After this has been tried for a while, it is worth deciding beforehand what is going to be picked up. For example, a Zone 1, white tip for a little finger with a short free edge (very small) and then a Zone 1 white tip for a middle finger with a medium-length free edge (considerably bigger), and so on.

By determining how big the bead needs to be before it is picked up will save so much time later and is part of the way towards creating a good structure with a brush and not correcting a bad structure with a buffer.

Condition of the liquid: During this little exercise, the condition of the liquid should be noted. If it is looking cloudy or if there is powder at the bottom of the dish, it is badly contaminated. If this liquid was used on a nail with a clear or pink overlay, it would look cloudy and mottled. This **contamination** must be avoided during working and is easily achieved. When working, the brush should be occasionaly dipped into the liquid and taken straight out without wiping it on the sides and wiped on to a disposable towel or tissue. This, if done a couple of times, will remove the build up of powder that accumulates in the hairs and then goes into the liquid. When using white-tip powder, the brush should always be cleaned in this way after each nail. This is because the powder will remain in the brush and the next time the brush is dipped in and pressed on the side the powder will be left in the liquid and the nails will become more and more cloudy. Some technicians even have a separate dish of liquid just for white-tip powder to prevent this happening.

Application on the nails: Once a certain amount of product control is achieved, then application on to the nails can start. This procedure is the same for a natural nail overlay.

- **Materials required**:
  – Clean terry towel on desk
  – Three layers of disposable towels
  – Tissues or disposable towels
  – Liquid monomer in clean, covered dappen dish
  – Powder polymers in clean, covered dappen dishes
  – Primer (if required)
  – Clean sable brush
  – Files of 240 grit
  – Oil
  – Buffers, such as a white block
  – Three-way buffer or block.

Note: zoning (that is applying the overlay in each zone) is the ideal application technique for this system. If white-tip powder is being used, the zoning principle is essential. By differentiating between Zone 2 and 3, the perfect structure can be created. However, applying the overlay in Zone 2 and 3 together is not wrong and, as long as the technician achieves the correct structure, the degree of zoning is a matter of choice.

- **Creating the perfect shape**: One of the most important aims of applying overlays is to create as close to the perfect shape as possible with the brush and not rely on correcting mistakes with a buffer afterwards. This obviously takes practise but should always be aimed for. Liquid and powder overlays continue to polymerize for quite some time after they become hard enough to buff. Too much buffing can interrupt the polymer chains being formed and create weak spots. Also, a great deal of time can be wasted by buffing away what has just been applied. It is much easier to try to apply it correctly in the first place and use the buffing as a refinement stage of the process.

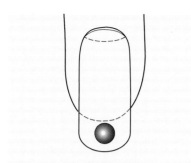

Bead placement for Zone 1

Angle of brush for Zone 1

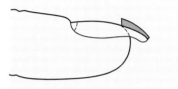

Shape of overlay in Zone 1

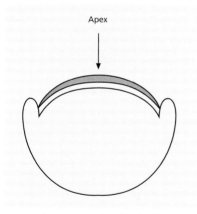

View of even overlay by looking down barrel of nail

Placement of bead for Zone 2

- **Application using white-tip powder:**
  1 The nails should have the tips perfectly blended, the dust removed and be clean and oil-free. One hand is worked on at a time from start to finish.
  2 Apply primer (if instructed by manufacturers) very sparingly around the base of the nail. Make sure the primer is dry before applying overlay.
  3 Clean the brush first by dipping it into the liquid, taking it straight out and wiping it on or between sheets of disposable towel.
  4 Start with the little finger, pick up a bead of white-tip powder that is approximately the right size and place it in the centre of Zone 1 closer to the smile line than the edge.
  5 Wipe the brush on the towel.
  6 Holding the brush at the same angle as the upper arch of the nail and with the tip of the brush, press the bead. Take part of the bead to one side wall and create the point of the smile line; take part of the bead to the other side wall and create the point of the smile line; create the smile line as neatly as possible with the tip of the brush and smooth the surface of the whole zone. If the brush is angled down slightly and the overlay is gently pushed up towards the smile line, a sharper line can be created and a thinner edge of the nail (see diagram). If the smile line is uneven and needs straightening, the extreme tip of the brush (cleaned and dry) can be used to do this making sure that the nail plate does not get monomer from the brush on it. Check the shape by looking down the barrel of the nail to make sure the overlay is even. The centre of this smile line will form the apex of the nail. (Some technicians like to apply white tip to each nail before Zone 2. This is usually to avoid contaminating the liquid. As the overlay starts polymerizing immediately the bond between the overlay at Zone 1 and 2 may have a weak point in it as Zone 1 has polymerized too much to blend with Zone 2. A stronger overlay is achieved if the whole nail is completed and contamination is easily avoided.)
  7 Clean the brush.
  8 Pick up a bead of pink or clear of the right size and place it in the centre of Zone 2 next to the white tip.
  9 Wipe the brush.
  10 The bead will have started to melt while wiping the brush and will be ready to press into shape. Making slow and deliberate movements and keeping the brush parallel with the nail, press the bead and, like Zone 1, take part of the bead out towards the side wall, leaving most in the centre and blend over the white tip, take part out to the other side wall and blend over the white tip. Blend the whole zone over the tip. Check down the barrel for evenness and thin sides.

11 Pick up a bead for Zone 3 and place it in the centre of the zone.

12 Wipe the brush.

13 Press the bead and blend up over the whole nail.

14 With the brush flattened, press the overlay towards the nail fold, taking great care not to touch the skin with the brush and leaving a tiny margin of bare nail bed. With the flattened brush between the overlay and the nail fold, gently press the overlay to thin the zone and create a good bond with the nail plate.

15 Check shape from both sides to make sure the upper arch is in place and the overlay is smooth. Check overlay from down the barrel.

16 Repeat process for each finger. Polymerization has occured when the overlay can be tapped with the handle of the brush and a 'clicking' sound can be heard. If the click sounds dull, it is not sufficiently cured. Discard towel that has been used to wipe brush.

17 When all nails on one hand are finished, go back to the little finger with a 240 grit file. Gently buff over the whole surface to smooth out any bumps and ridges. Carefully blend the edges of the overlay making sure the tiny margin of exposed nail plate is not buffed. Check overlay from all angles to ensure a perfect structure. Refine the free edge to make it as thin and even as possible.

18 Repeat for all nails.

19 Return to little finger and buff whole surface with a white block as this will start to refine the surface ready for final stage.

20 Repeat for all fingers.

21 Using a three-way buffer in the correct sequence (usually black, white then grey) buff all nails to a high-gloss shine without any dull spots (dips in the overlay).

22 Remove all the dust, including that which has collected under the nail and discard layer of disposable towel with all the dust.

23 Apply oil to each nail and massage into nail and cuticle.

24 Repeat whole process to other hand.

25 When both hands are completed tidy desk by cleaning brush thoroughly and storing flat and away from dust, discard any unused monomer onto the disposable towel remaining on the desk. Make sure powder dishes are covered. Wipe surface of the desk with cloth dampened with a mild disinfectant and prepare for next client with clean towels, etc.

• If the overlay is being applied without white tip, it should be applied in zones but it would not be necessary to create a smile line. Otherwise the process is the same.

Angle of brush for Zone 2

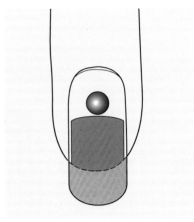

Placement of bead for Zone 3

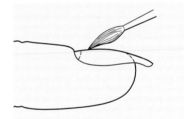

Angle of brush for Zone 3

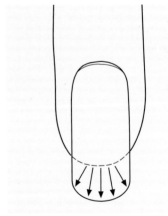

Refine free edge with 240 grit buffer

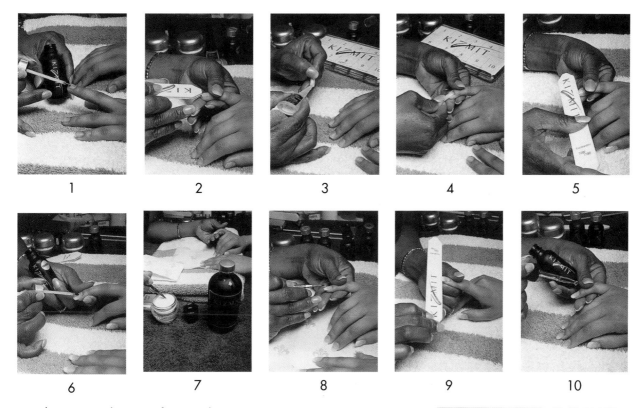

Step-by-step application of an acrylic system
1 Sanitize and dehydrate the natural nail plate
2 Remove shine from nail plate, shape the free edge and dehydrate
3 Select correct tip
4 Apply tip to natural nail, avoiding bubbles under contact area
5 Cut and shape tip; blend to natural nail
6 Apply small amount of primer to centre of nail and allow to dry to a chalky white appearance
7 Immerse clean acrylic brush in liquid monomer; wipe away excess liquid; gently place the tip of the brush onto the surface of the powder and pick up a medium-sized bead of product
8 Place the bead onto the nail; apply medium pressure to form the desired shape of the free edge; repeat steps 7 and 8 three more times to cover all zones of the nail, avoiding contact with the skin and cuticle area
9 File, shape and buff to a high-shine finish
10 Apply recommended oil to each cuticle and emollient to hands and massage well
11 Finished nails

Trouble shooting: If the overlay looks powdery in Zone 3, it is usually because the client's hands are very cold or the liquid monomer is cold. This hinders the rate of polymerization leaving unpolymerized powder on the surface. This can be corrected by warming the client's hands before application or making sure that the monomer is at room temperature before using. If it is an emergency, for example, the first client of the day in a salon that has not yet warmed up, the covered dappen dish with the monomer can be placed in a bowl of tepid water (not hot) to bring it to room temperature.

If the brush to be used was not cleaned properly after the last use and has a lump of product in it, soften the product in some monomer (not anything else) and use a paper towel to try to remove the debris, do not use fingers as a sensitivity to the product will result. An orange stick can be used to dislodge the debris but this will usually result in damaged hairs and a brush that does not work very well. Discard the monomer that was used.

UV gel

This system is often considered to be one of the easiest to learn for a beginner. This is possibly true as, once the tips have been applied, there is a very easy method of applying a UV gel as an overlay. The artificial nails produced by this method are not necessarily very strong as it does not create a structure with the curves that produce a very strong nail. This would be suitable for those who will wear their nails quite short or are used to having long nails and therefore unlikely to break them.

There are many different types of gels on the market now and technology in this area has advanced a great deal in the last few years. There is such a choice of gels now that a skilled technician can do everything that can be done with a liquid and powder system.

The gel 'system': Gels now come in all colours and the gel 'system' can comprise a single component – that is, one type of gel – or it can comprise several gel components, all of which are recommended as being needed to create an artificial nail. Like all other systems, the choice is down to personal preference and cost.

- Gels can be called a 'pre-mixed' system as all the gel needs to polymerize is UV light rather than another product or chemical. Although all gels are still in the acrylate family, there seem to be two distinct types of gel in use. The first is self-levelling and the second is non self-levelling.
- The bonds in gels are very strong and this usually makes them resistant to solvents. If this is the case, as it is with many gels, the overlay cannot be 'soaked' off and requires buffing to remove it. Depending on company marketing, this can be a benefit or hazard. A solvent-resistant overlay is definitely resistant to damage and discoloration from nail varnish and remover.
- Soaking nails in a solvent to remove them is very drying to the nail plate and surrounding skin and the nail plate especially takes time to recover from this major dehydration. Oils and moisturizers can be used after removal if artificial nails are not being replaced to help this recovery. Occasional rumours arise in the industry suggesting that this method can be damaging to health. All chemicals are damaging to health if an individual is overexposed, and the overexposure level to the solvents used in this industry, such as acetone, is very high (see Chapter 9).

- Removing artificial nails by buffing needs skill and this can be achieved only by practise on real fingers. At first, it can be time-consuming and, when done improperly, can cause severe damage to the nail plate if overbuffed. Ideally, the removal of nails should be a rare occurence and should happen only when the client does not want artificial nails any more.
- There are some gels on the market now that can be removed with solvents so these can give the same choice of removal method as the other systems.
- A word of warning about coloured gels (and acrylics): an opaque overlay could be hiding a problem! If lifting has occurred or if the nail plate or nail bed has become infected, it will not be seen. The only way to ensure this is not happening is to remove the overlay at very regular intervals which, in itself, could cause a problem. Belief that the overlay will not lift is not sufficient as a client may be resistant to any overlay, or may become resistant at any time owing to a change in the nail plate.
- With a one-component gel system, the gel is applied to the nail in one or more layers to build up strength. In a two- or three- or more-component system, there is usually a gel that acts as a bonding layer; it is compatible with the nail plate and also with the next layer of gel; next there is a thick gel that can build an overlay with the required structure, that is curves, and then a sealer gel that provides a high-gloss shine and protection. Manufacturers' instructions should always be followed.

Application of the nails:

- **Materials required**:
  - Clean terry towel on desk
  - Three layers of disposable towels
  - Tissues or disposable towels
  - Gels
  - UV lamp
  - Primer (if required)
  - Clean brush, either nylon or natural hair
  - Finishing wipe (if required)
  - Files of 240 grit
  - Oil
  - Buffers, such as a white block
  - Three-way buffer (if required).
- **Application**: Both hands are worked on at the same time with this system:
  1 Both hands, with tips applied, must be clean and totally dust-free (gels are very susceptible to dust as it causes a lumpy overlay).
  2 Apply primer to Zone 3, if required, and allow to dry.
  3 Open gel and, with a clean brush, apply a thin layer of gel to each nail, taking care not to touch soft tissue (remove

with orange stick if this happens). The gel is applied in this method like painting with nail varnish but bring the brush to the edge of the nail and wipe downwards off the edge. This will help to seal the edge and prevent any shrinkage of the overlay. If a 'whole-hand' lamp is being used then include the thumb, otherwise, just apply gel to the four fingers.

4 Turn on lamp and ask client to place fingers under the lamp, making sure that the fingers are correctly placed and all are exposed to the UV light. This usually takes 2 minutes, but refer to instructions.

5 While the first hand is under the lamp, repeat the process to the other hand.

6 Remove the first hand and replace with the second.

7 If a small lamp is being used, the thumb will need to have the overlay applied now and then it can replace the second hand after the cure time.

8 Repeat for thumb of second hand.

9 Apply second layer of gel to nails of first hand while second thumb is under lamp and cure.

10 Repeat until all fingers of both hands have had second layer.

11 If the nails are long or if the client is heavy on her hands, it may be necessary to add a third layer in the same way.

12 When all nails have had sufficient layers applied and they have been cured, replace lid of gel and clean brush with nail varnish remover, or equivalent, on a tissue.

13 Many gels have a sticky surface layer that is uncured monomer. This must be removed and most brands have a product that will do this job efficiently without damaging the gel. The monomer must be kept off the skin at this stage so a new nail wipe or equivalent must be used for each nail and the nail must be wiped from the nail fold towards the tip. By doing this there is little chance of the monomer touching the skin. If the same wipe is used, monomer from the previous nail will come into contact with the skin and the client will develop a sensitivity eventually and be unable to wear the artificial nails. The monomer must be thoroughly removed as any remaining will be in the dust created at the next stage and will touch the skin of both the client and the technician.

14 It is possible to leave the nails exactly as they are now if they look a perfect shape; however, there are often small imperfections in the surface and sometimes the gel will have shrunk slightly and the extreme tip looks more rounded than it should.

15 If the nails need refining, a very soft file should be used or a white block as the surface of a gel is usually quite soft. The shape should be checked from all sides.

16 At this stage there are two options: the nails can be buffed with a three-way buffer which will produce a natural shine

(not a high shine as the surface is usually too soft) or a thin layer of the gel can be applied and cured to produce a high gloss after the sticky layer is removed. If the second option is chosen, all the dust created by the buffing must be carefully removed with the finishing wipe on a tissue and the paper towel removed with all the dust that has collected.

17 Apply oil and massage.

18 Clean desk and prepare for next client.

- **Structuring method with a thicker gel**:
    1 Both hands, with tips applied, must be clean and totally dust-free (gels are very susceptible to dust as it causes a lumpy overlay).

    2 Apply primer to Zone 3, if required, and allow to dry or apply bonding gel if appropriate and cure for recommended time.

    3 Open gel and, with a clean brush, apply a bead of gel to the centre of the nail at where the apex should be. Take part of the bead to the side wall at the stress area and take part of the bead to the other side wall at the stress area. Ease part of the bead down towards the nail fold, taking care not to touch the skin. Bring part of the bead with the brush to the edge of the nail and wipe downwards off the edge. This will help to seal the edge and prevent any shrinkage of the overlay. The gel should now have a thin layer at the free edge in Zone 1, a thicker layer at the stress area in Zone 2 and a thin layer in Zone 3. The surface now needs gently smoothing over with featherlight movements of the brush until the shape is right from all angles. If a 'whole-hand' lamp and a gel that does not run is being used then include the thumb, otherwise, just apply gel to the four fingers.

    4 Turn on lamp and ask client to place fingers under the lamp, making sure that the fingers are correctly placed and all are exposed to the UV light. This usually takes 2 minutes, but refer to instructions. It is possible that a heat reaction may be felt by the client. Polymerization is an 'exothermic' chemical reaction (gives off heat) and the reaction in a gel is usually very fast. If the gel layer is thick or if the client has thin or sensitive nail beds the heat may be felt. The client should be warned that this may happen and to help avoid it, the fingers should be placed under the light for 5 seconds, then removed for 5 seconds. This should be repeated at least once more and the heat sensation, if it is going to happen, may be avoided. If the heat is felt, and it is usually quite sudden, tell the client to remove her fingers and press them on the desk very firmly. This will stop the reaction and then the fingers can be replaced.

5 While the first hand is under the lamp, repeat the process to the other hand.

6 Remove the first hand and replace with the second.

7 If a small lamp is being used or a gel that can run, the thumb will need to have the overlay applied now and then it can replace the second hand after the cure time.

8 Repeat for thumb of second hand.

9 When all nails have had sufficient layers applied and they have been cured, replace lid of gel and clean brush with the finishing wipe, or equivalent, on a tissue.

10 Many gels have a sticky surface layer that is uncured monomer. This must be removed and most brands have a product that will do this job efficiently without damaging the gel. The monomer must be kept off the skin at this stage so a new nail wipe or equivalent must be used for each nail and the nail must be wiped from the nail fold towards the tip. By doing this there is little chance of the monomer touching the skin. If the same wipe is used, monomer from the previous nail will come into contact with the skin and the client will develop a sensitivity eventually and be unable to wear the artificial nails. The monomer must be thoroughly removed as any remaining will be in the dust created at the next stage and will touch the skin of both the client and the technician.

11 The nails now need refining as there are often small imperfections in the surface and sometimes the gel will have shrunk slightly and the extreme tip looks more rounded than it should. The structure should also be checked to make sure it is correct and the same on each nail.

12 A very soft file should be used as the surface of a gel is usually quite soft. The shape should be checked from all sides.

13 At this stage there are two options: the nails can be buffed with a three-way buffer which will produce a natural shine (not a high shine as the surface is usually too soft) or a thin layer of the gel can be applied and cured to produce a high gloss after the sticky layer is removed. If the second option is chosen, all the dust created by the buffing must be carefully removed with the finishing wipe on a tissue and the paper towel removed with all the dust that has collected.

14 Apply oil and massage.

15 Clean desk and prepare for next client.

The fibre system

This is a relatively easy system and relies heavily on the skilful application of the tips. Owing to the nature of the products, it is not possible to create any additional curves in the overlay as can be done with a liquid and powder or a thick gel. Therefore the shape of the finished nail relies on the shape of the tip. It is

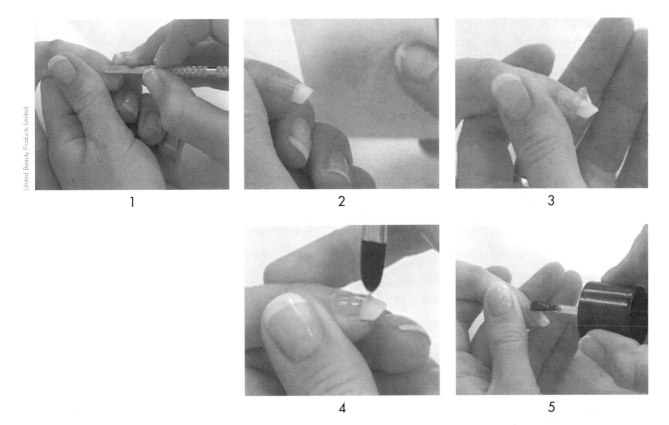

1   2   3

4   5

Step-by-step application of a thicker-style UV gel application technique
1 Prepare the nail by carefully removing all traces of cuticle from the nail plate and then dehydrating
2 Choose a tip that fits the finger perfectly, apply it and blend to the natural nail; remove all dust
3 Pick up a bead of the UV gel and place in the centre of the nail over the stress area
4 Gently move the gel into the correct structure for the nail and smooth the surface of the overlay before curing; follow the manufacturer's instructions with regard to curing under UV light
5 When cured, remove any sticky layer as instructed and shape overlay with a soft file; remove all dust and apply a gloss sealer if appropriate

possible to build in a little extra strength with the fibre but this is relatively minimal.

There are fewer actual brands of this system on the market – that is, a collection of products that make a full system under one name – than the other systems, but the individual components are readily available.

- **Mesh and resin**: There is a choice of silk or fibreglass to use as the mesh. The resin used in this system is sometimes called a **'no-light' gel**. This should not be confused with a UV gel. A 'no-light' gel in this system is a cyanoacrylate resin that is slightly thicker and more like a gel in consistency. (It is, however, possible to use fibre with a UV gel as an added strength or in free-form sculpting.) There are also two different methods to 'activate' the resin, with a spray **activator** or a brush-on activator. Both are effective and are usually very similar chemicals. It is a matter of choice but a brush-on version obviously avoids chemicals being vaporized in the air that can cause a higher incidence of sensitivity developing in individuals.

- **Materials required**:
  - Several layers of disposable towels
  - Nail wipes or cotton wool
  - Fibre scissors that have a very fine and very sharp blade
  - Fibre mesh, silk or fibreglass kept in a plastic cover or box
  - Resin with long nozzle
  - Activator, spray or brush on
  - 240 grit files
  - White block
  - Three-way buffer
  - Oil.

- **Application**:
  1 One hand is worked on at a time from start to finish.
  2 The nails with tips must be clean and dehydrated. (This system does not require any primer and the rough surface of the nail plate is enough to hold the overlay.)
  3 Using the scissors and avoiding handling the fibre too much, cut a piece of fibre that is the approximate width of the nail to be overlayed.
  4 Remove the fibre from its paper backing and use the backing to hold the fibre while it is put in place.
  5 Place the fibre onto the nail close to but not touching the nail fold. Use the backing paper to press the fibre onto the length of the nail. Avoid touching it with fingers as they will leave behind a small amount of moisture and this will prevent the resin from soaking into the mesh. Trim the sides if necessary by sliding the blade of the scissors down the side wall and cutting the excess. Trim the excess length of fibre by angling the scissors backwards on the nail tip so the fibre is cut slightly shorter than the tip. This allows the end to be sealed with the resin. (If the artificial nail needs extra strength, a strip of fibre can be placed across the stress area. This can either be a strip placed on the nail before this stage, or it can be a double layer of the fibre, see diagram.)
  6 Repeat this for all fingers excluding thumb.
  7 Apply a very small amount of resin down the centre of the nail and, with the side of the nozzle, use little circular movements to spread the resin over the nail and work it into the mesh. More resin can be applied if necessary but, at this stage, the pattern of the mesh should still be visible but very wet.
  8 Repeat for all fingers.
  9 Go back to little finger and apply a very small amount of resin down the centre of the nail and spread it over whole nail with side of nozzle. (It will not need spreading if a brush-on activator is being used.) Take great care not to touch the skin and to leave a tiny margin of bare nail around the edges. Seal the tip of the nail with the side of the nozzle. (If too much resin is applied, it will run into the side walls.)
  10 Repeat for all fingers.

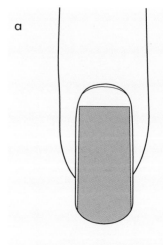

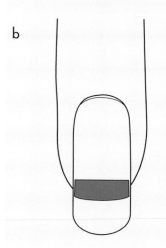

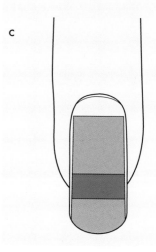

Placing fibre on stress area
a Single layer of fibre
b Stress strip of fibre
c Overlapped fibre in stress area

11 If a spray activator is being used, hold it at least 12 inches away from the nails and spray once (ensuring the aim is right!). The resin needs only minute amounts of a spray activator. If too much is sprayed or it is too close, a sudden heat reaction will occur that is very painful for the client and can ruin the overlay.

12 If a brush-on activator is being used, it will need its brush cleaner at the ready. (The brushes in this type of product can get stuck with polymerized resin and need to be put in a solvent between uses to keep them clean. It is usual to have another bottle of a similar size and shape that has the solvent and a spare brush in it so they can be alternated during applications.) Spread the resin with the activator brush to cover the nail while keeping the product off the skin and leaving a tiny margin around the edge. This will mix the activator into the resin and speed up the polymerization process. (This activator is usually much weaker than the spray version, so the process is slower.)

13 Repeat for all fingers with more activator on the brush for each finger. Replace brush in activator bottle.

14 Apply another layer of resin to all fingers and either spread with nozzle or leave for brush.

15 Activate in the same way as before.

16 Repeat whole procedure from Step 3 on thumb.

17 Another layer of resin may be applied if more strength is required.

18 (If brush-on activator is being used, remove spare brush from the solvent and wipe it on a paper towel to remove most of the solvent. Wipe the brush that has just been used on the paper towel and place it in the solvent. Put the spare brush into the activator bottle ready for the next use.)

19 The overlay should be relatively smooth and should need minimal buffing to refine and smooth the surface. If the activator has been sprayed too close, there may be pits in the surface that will need buffing out. (If this happens and by removing them the overlay is made too thin, the nail should be cleaned of dust and a layer replaced.)

20 Refine the surface further with a white block.

21 Bring the nails to a high shine with a three-way buffer.

22 Remove all dust and apply oil.

This nail system is not solvent-resistant at all. If nail varnish is to be worn then a very gentle remover should be used otherwise the surface will be destroyed. If varnish is removed many times, the whole nail may be undermined.

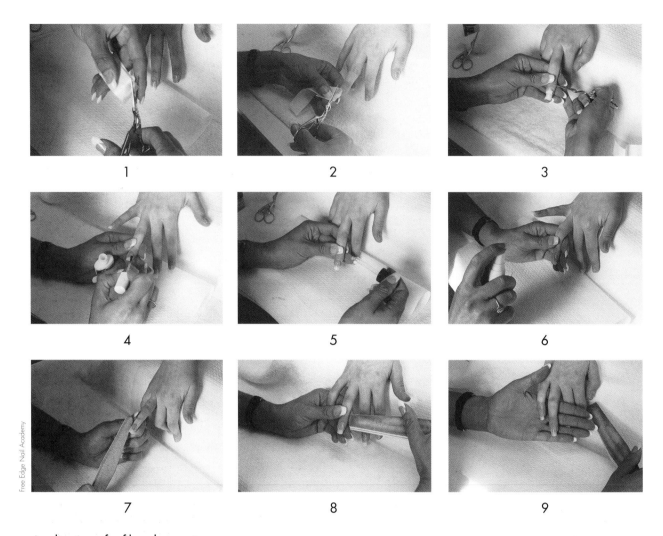

Free Edge Nail Academy

Application of a fibreglass system
1 Cut corner off mesh to allow for a close fit
2 Place the mesh on the nail
3 Cut off end of mesh that is overhanging and place over stress zone to enhance and strengthen this zone
4 Apply brush on resin over entire surface
5 Drop activator to set the resin…
6 … Or spray to activate curing process
7 File and shape nail
8 Buff to shine
9 Finished fibre nail

Creating the natural-looking nail

A nail correctly applied in one system should not look widely different from one applied in another. The white tip that can be used in an acrylic system may look different from others but there are white gels available and the fibre system can use French white tips.

The finish can sometimes look different and a gel with high gloss looks different from a high shine achieved by buffing an acrylic. However, if the high gloss is preferred by a client who wears acrylic nails, the gloss gel can be applied to an acrylic to give it that effect.

When applying nails, the most important aim is to create a natural-looking nail that suits the hand and is the strongest structure it can be. A technician is only as good as their last set of nails. No one can create perfection every time and a beginner needs to be able to look at their results and recognize what can be improved. An eye for balance and symmetry is not always a natural skill and needs to be learned. A trainee technician who has the skill naturally is very lucky; most do not have it and need to develop it. Many are not even aware that it is missing and send clients out with very strange shapes on their fingers.

PROBLEM SHAPES

Following on from problem shapes encountered in Chapter 6 on tip application, there are some shapes that can be improved by the overlay.

Ski-jump nails

If the tip is put on at the correct angle for a ski-jump nail, the lower arch will be good but the upper arch will be very strange. This can be very easily corrected by careful structuring of the overlay to create a good upper arch and a strong nail (see diagram).

Bitten nails

Still the most difficult problem to overcome, like the ski-jump, the bitten nail can be further improved by the overlay as it has a similar problem. The overlay only has a tiny nail plate to hold on to and the length must be just to the end of the finger, but, the overlay can be applied so that the upper arch can look quite natural. The nail really needs to be covered with coloured varnish to hide the lack of smile line but, if this is done the finished nail will look very good.

Twisted nails

If natural nails were allowed to continue growing, they would curve down and twist in a clockwise or anticlockwise direction. These twists may not start until the nail has reached a decent length, but they may start quite definitely on the nail bed. This can be seen if the shape of the barrel is viewed from either the tip looking towards the hand or from the hand looking towards the tip. It is difficult to see if the nail plate is very short but the longer the nail is the more obvious the twisting becomes. Once a tip is applied and blended a twist may become obvious. The lower arches will be uneven with one side dipping down more than the other. This can be easily rectified during the blending of the tip by matching both sides of the lower arch. The twist of the barrel can be rectified by placing slightly more product on one side than the other and making the 'C' curve of the nail even. The additional

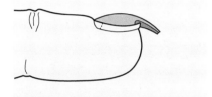

Tip blended and overlay applied to correct poor upper arch

Tip cut short and blended with overlay to compensate for poor shape

product is minimal and it is very easy to overcompensate. The easiest way to see this is by turning the client's hand around and looking down the nail from the hand down to the tip.

PRACTISE MAKES PERFECT

Applying artificial nails is not just about making nails longer. It is also a skill that can solve many problems and make imperfect nails look perfect. By understanding the systems and becoming skilful at creating shapes a technician can do many things with artificial nails. It is possible to replace nail plates that have been lost through accident or illness. It is possible to rebuild nails that are deformed through damage or an heriditary factor. It is even possible to build a nail where one does not exist, such as where the tip of the finger is missing. (If any work like this is attempted with a client who has a medical condition, it is important to get approval from their doctor first.)

The secret of the true professional and successful technician is *practise*. No technician can practise too much, both in perfecting shape and product control and applying perfect nails to every client regardless of nail shape, condition and lifestyle. When practising, technicians should aim to be capable of applying a full set of artificial nail extensions in under 2 hours. This is acceptable for a client receiving a treatment from a technician, as opposed to a trainee. Every technician should aim to provide a full set of artificial nails in $1^1/_2$ hours or less.

Some nail salons work very well on the fact that every treatment can be carried out in 1 hour or less. This is the choice of the salon and their clients and can work very well if all hygiene rules, working practices and client care are maintained. Other salons, on the other hand, prefer to give their clients more time and relaxation. The most important aspect of every treatment is *safety* and *quality*.

SUMMARY

This chapter has first examined the function and structure of overlays and then demonstrated step-by-step techniques for their application to create a natural-looking nail whichever system – liquid and powder, UV gel or fibre – the technician has used.

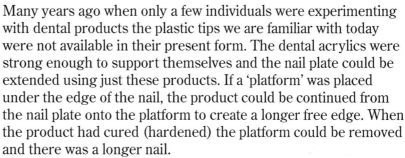

CHAPTER 8

The Art and Skill of Applying Sculptured Nails

INTRODUCTION

This chapter looks in step-by-step detail at applying sculptured nails.

SCULPTURED NAILS OR PLASTIC TIPS?

A selection of forms

Many years ago when only a few individuals were experimenting with dental products the plastic tips we are familiar with today were not available in their present form. The dental acrylics were strong enough to support themselves and the nail plate could be extended using just these products. If a 'platform' was placed under the edge of the nail, the product could be continued from the nail plate onto the platform to create a longer free edge. When the product had cured (hardened) the platform could be removed and there was a longer nail.

This method is generally called 'free-form sculpture' or **sculptured nails** and there are many different versions of specially designed 'platforms' that are called 'forms', the choice is a matter of personal preference. Many technicians learned how to do 'nails' in this way only and many still prefer this method to the method of applying plastic tips first. Applying artificial nails in this way is very skilful but then so is applying tips correctly. The method misses out the whole stage of tip application but needs some time spent on placing the chosen form in exactly the right place. On balance, a technician skilled in sculpting nails can complete a set in a shorter length of time than a set using tips.

The results of the two methods rely entirely on the skill of the technician. For many, artificial nails with a tip will result in a stronger nail, but only if the tip is applied perfectly and there are no weak areas around the smile line, the blending or the side walls. A sculpting technician can produce a perfect nail that does not have any of these weak spots either. This can be difficult as there will often be a step created where the form meets the nail plate and some product can seep under the free edge. If there is

United Beauty Products Ltd

no natural free edge, there may be a step up where the form does not meet the free edge. A sculptured nail must also have sufficient strength at the side walls without looking too thick otherwise the free edge will snap off very easily. All of these features can be achieved by skilful application.

SYSTEMS AND FORMS

Systems

The liquid and powder system is the one most commonly used to create sculptured nails as its application and **curing** methods suit the way the nail is achieved. UV gel is also used as the thicker gels will stay in place on a form for UV curing to take place, and with the coloured gels a white tip can be achieved. The fibre system is rarely used in this way. It is possible to hold the fibre before the excess length has been removed and coat it with the resin. This will result in extra length without a tip, but it is very delicate and would not last very long. It would also be clear and would need coloured varnish to disguise it.

Forms

There are many different types of forms available. Some are *disposable* and used from a roll. These have a sticky back and this allows them to be held in place on the finger. Technicians have all sorts of inventive ways of shaping these to help produce the perfect nail. They are used for one nail and then discarded. They usually have a metallic finish of some description as this will reflect back the small amount of heat polymerization produces and ensures the under-surface of the free edge is fully cured. With UV cured materials, it is usually worth removing the form after curing and replacing the fingers under the light with the palm of the hand upwards to make sure the underside is cured.

Together with disposable forms there are also an array of *reusable* forms of different shapes and sizes. Like many things in the art of applying artificial nails, the decision which one to use is a matter of personal choice. The forms, both disposable and reusable, do not cost much money so it is worth trying out as many as possible to see which is preferred. It is also worth having several types as some will fit a specific nail shape better than others and this will make the fitting of the form much quicker.

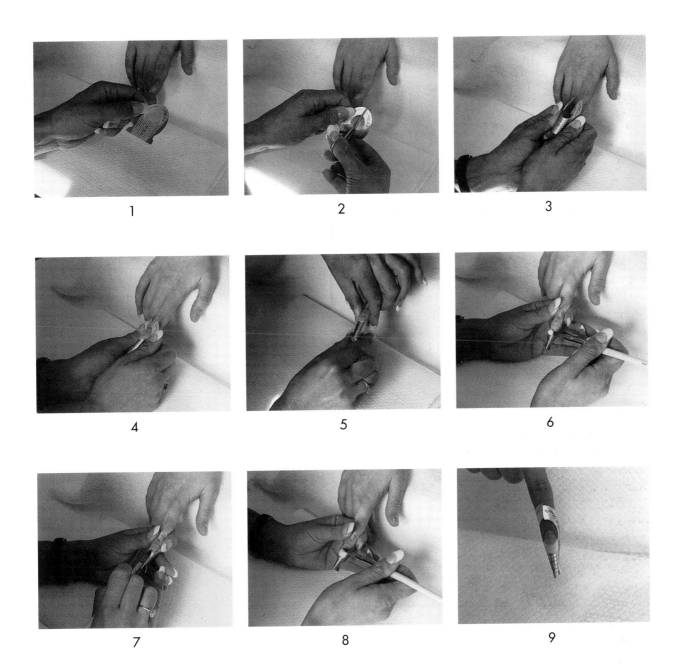

Sculptured Nails
1 Select form
2 Cut form to allow for movement and splaying form for perfect fit
3 Fit form
4 Secure side of form
5 Pinch in end of form to create C curve
6 1st bead placement
7 Work free edge
8 2nd bead placement – creating body of nail
9 Sculpt complete

continues

10

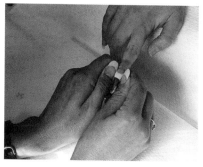

11

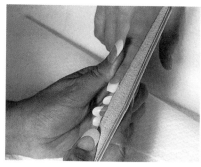

12

13

14

15

Sculptured Nails (continued)
10 Remove form
11 Pinch lateral walls for optimum C curve just prior to polymerization
12 Shape nail
13 Bevel free edge
14 Buff to high shine
15 Finished nail

CHAPTER 9

Maintaining Artificial Nails

INTRODUCTION

Every client is a 'full-set' client once; after that, they become a maintenance client or a natural nail client. Skilful maintenance is as important as skilful application and will keep clients returning on a regular basis. This chapter explores in depth the value and techniques of a regular maintenance programme and examines the most common diseases and disorders the technician may have to deal with.

VALUE OF MAINTENANCE

During training, maintenance is one of the most useful learning aids and must never be dismissed or skipped over. Many hours can be spent on learning application skills but every client is different and every set of circumstances is different. A trainee technician will learn nothing if they do not see the results of their application a few weeks later. The preparation of the nail may have been incomplete; the client may have a nail plate that is more oily than expected; the ratio of the product may have been wrong; the shape that looked good two weeks ago now looks horrible.

It is a fact that more is often learned from a mistake or something that goes wrong than anything else. It is not enough for a trainer to explain what 'may' happen. It is essential that the beginner can see *what* has happened and try to work out *why* it has happened. If this is done with the help of a trainer then, when the technician is on their own with a client who has a problem, they will be able to work out why and how to put it right.

Like hair, nails are continually growing and what was put onto a nail near to the nail fold will be in a different place in two weeks' time. This is obvious if coloured nail varnish is worn for some time. There will be a gap at the base of the nail and that small area of exposed nail plate will probably have cuticle attached to it. Just as in hairdressing, when hair has been coloured or permed, the 'regrowth' is very obvious.

NEED FOR REGULAR MAINTENANCE

The appearance of an outgrown artificial nail is one consideration, but there are two more important reasons for regular maintenance treatments:

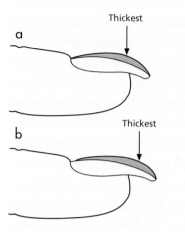

1 The technician will have explained to their client that they must watch out for any *changes to the nail*, and return immediately if anything is noticed. However, it is possible that there may be very slight changes that the client has not noticed, especially if coloured varnish has been worn. There may be some lifting of the overlay that is not very obvious. There may be a slight reaction to the products. There may be some minor nail separation owing to thin or dehydrated nail plates that was not evident before. It is important that the technician keeps a close watch on the health of the nails and skin as they should know things to look for that may not be so obvious to the untrained eye.

Nail growth
a Position of overlay at application stage
b Position of overlay at 2 weeks' growth

2 After a period of natural nail growth, the structure that was created during application that had the two curves (upper arch and 'C' curve) meeting at the apex or stress point of the nail to create the strongest nail possible will have moved. The apex will have moved further away from the nail bed and could be on the free edge. This will unbalance the nail and make it susceptible to breakages. The smile line that was created either by the tip application or by a white tip overlay will also have moved and there will be a band of natural nail growth that will be a different colour to the tip.

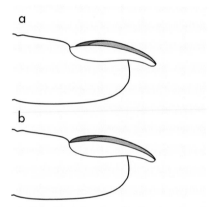

Infill procedure
a Buff overlay near cuticle
b Replace overlay in shaded area

MAINTENANCE TREATMENTS

Infill or rebalance?

There are two types of maintenance treatments. One, called an **'infill'**, is a short treatment that allows the technician to check for any problems and fill in the small area of growth to make the artificial nail look smooth without a ridge at the base. The other is called a **'rebalance'**, as it removes the apex that has moved to the wrong place and replaces it in the right place, it fills the regrowth area at the base and, if required, will put the smile line back to where it should be and cover the band of natural nail growth.

The decision as to which treatment is needed should depend on the rate of nail growth. If it is slow to average, it is likely that an 'infill' will be required 2 weeks after the first application and a 'rebalance' 2 weeks after that. These treatments can then be alternated. If nail growth is average to fast, then a full rebalance may be needed every 2–3 weeks. Every client is different but the guideline is 2 weeks between treatments. This must be shorter for a nail biter who must be seen at 1-week intervals for several weeks. Some clients may settle down to a treatment every 3–4 weeks if they have a slow nail growth and are used to having long nails.

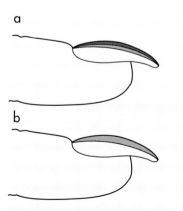

Rebalance procedure
a Remove most of overlay
b Replace with complete overlay

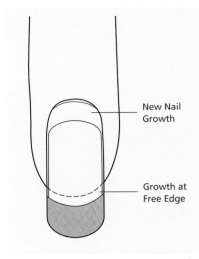

'Smile line' at 2 weeks' growth; must be replaced to correct area

Assessment of client's nails

Before the maintenance treatment can start, the technician must look very carefully at the client's nails, especially if it is the first maintenance visit after application of a first full set. This is especially true for trainees and beginners and much will be learned from spending some time at this stage.

The aim for every technician is to see a set of nails return looking perfect except for the small growth area at the base and at the smile line. Experienced technicians will achieve this with the vast majority of new clients and all existing clients. Beginners will experience all kinds of problems that will need solving during the first year but must never accept that this is part of wearing artificial nails. The saying of 'no pain, no gain' is most definitely not true in this case and, with skill and understanding, nearly every client should be able to wear beautiful and natural-looking nails without ever encountering a problem.

The incidence of an allergic reaction is probably the most worrying but the chance of this happening to even the most sensitive client can be minimized, if not totally avoided, by good working practices.

Procedure to follow

As trainees can learn a great deal at maintenance treatments it is a good idea to follow a set procedure. The differences between the systems at this stage is minimal.

What did the client want to achieve?

When providing a maintenance treatment, always remember what the client wanted to achieve at the beginning. Did they want to grow their own nails as soon as possible or were they happy to have artificial nails, long term? Did they want to grow the tips off and have natural nails with an overlay? European women, generally speaking, tend to prefer natural nails or, at least, artificial nails that look natural. They also tend to like to have the choice of reverting to natural nails at any time. Some do follow what seems to be more accepted in America, in that it is acceptable to have artificial nails that look artificial. This is a very wide generalization, but many more women in America have their nails done. Products have improved from the harsh dental acrylics that used to be used and technical skills are improving as awareness of the industry grows. Now there is no excuse not to keep the natural nail perfectly healthy and in at least the same condition as when artificial nails were first applied.

Is the client happy?

There should be discussion with the client as to how they are getting on and if they are happy with their nails. It may be that the original plan needs changing to achieve another goal. It is not unknown for a client to admit that they cannot cope with artificial nails or cannot afford long-term maintenance. If this is the case, the nails should be removed and a course of manicures suggested. The client should always feel that the choice is theirs and the technician's main aim is to provide them with what they want and take care of their natural nails, whatever the treatment may be. Many clients like the idea that their natural nails are growing healthily and protected under the artificial covering and, when the natural nail has grown to a good length, the artificial nail can be removed. This should be true for many clients if their natural nails are capable of growing in a reasonable shape. If this is the aim then the length of the nail should stay the same as the first application and infills and rebalances carried out. When the natural nail reaches the desired length, it is a natural nail with an overlay (the tip has grown out). The overlay can be infilled but thinned on successive visits until the overlay is as thin as possible or not needed at all.

Step-by-step approach

At the start of each maintenance treatment, four steps should be followed, then nothing of importance will be missed out:

Observation: Look carefully at all the nails. A perfect, trouble-free set should look tidy. The only difference from when they were first applied should be the natural nail growth at the cuticle, leaving a gap, and at the free edge with an obvious growth of natural nail. If there is anything more than this, there is a problem that needs solving and correcting and what is noticed should be noted on the record card. The shape of the artificial nail may not look as attractive as it did originally. It may look a bit bulbous at the sides or on the end. This will be due to the fact that the overlay was not applied in the best shape and was, perhaps a bit thick at the side walls.

Questioning: The client needs to be asked how they have managed with the nails. If there are any broken, ask how it happened. If it happened easily then the structure may not have been strong enough. If it happened during a minor incident and was painful, the structure was strong enough but maybe the nail was too long. If it happened during a minor accident, then any nails would probably have broken.

Diagnosing: If they are less than perfect, the technician needs to decide what the possible causes of the problem may be and discuss it with the client. The probable causes of the problem should be explained.

Treatment: Having followed the above steps, the most appropriate treatment can be decided upon and suggested to the client. If the nails are perfect, maintenance will be minimal. If, however, some are lost, broken or lifting, they will need replacing in such a way that the problem will not reoccur.

Putting right the problem

It is essential to be able to understand why the problem occurred, and how to put it right. As a guide, some common problems have been listed, with their possible causes and treatment. It is impossible to list every problem as every client is different but understanding of the system, its basic chemistry and the anatomy and physiology of the nail should provide the tools to be able to reach a logical conclusion. The solution to these problems is often termed 'contra-actions' as they are actions taken in response to a condition or situation.

Broken nails (if some product is left on the remaining nail plate)

Reason	Solution
1 Too long	Shorten all nails
2 Weak	Rebuild stress area

Missing nails (nothing is left on nail plate)

Reason	Solution
1 Oil or moisture on nail plate	Careful preparation
2 Client picking nails	Discussion

Lifting in Zone 3

Reason	Solution
1 Cuticle on nail	Careful preparation
2 Oil on nail	Careful preparation *or* 2nd coat of primer
3 Overlay too thin	Add *slightly* more
4 Overlay too thick	Refine overlay in Zone 3
5 Overlay touching skin	Take more care in application

Chipping at cuticle

Reason	Solution
1 Overlay too thick	Apply smaller beads
2 Overlay too brittle	Use wetter ratio in liquid and powder system
	Use less activator for fibre
3 Client picking	Discussion

Chipping at free edge

Reason	Solution
1 Overlay too brittle	Use wetter ratio or less activator
2 Overlay too thin	Apply more but taper

Discoloration of overlay

Reason	Solution
1 Contamination	Use fresh product and clean tools
2 Affected by UV light	Cover with UV-resistant sealer
3 Coloured varnish	Use base coat under varnish

Discoloration under overlay on nail plate: yellow–green

1 Fungal/bacterial infection	If very superficial (that is very pale colour and small area), remove overlay, dehydrate, prime and reapply; see client 1 week later If more serious, remove overlay and refer to GP/pharmacist

Discoloration under nail plate: yellow, green, white

Reason	Solution
1 Possible infection	Remove artificial nail and refer to GP

Discoloration under nail plate at free edge: white

- This is nail separation and may be caused by a number of different reasons. Correct treatment would be to remove all products and, if the condition is very minor wait and see if it improves. However, with experience, it may be possible to decide if it has occurred owing to a very thin nail plate that may have been caused by overbuffing previously (either by a bad technician or the client). A thinned nail can break the seal at the hyponychium and this can allow bacteria to enter under the nail plate. If the nail is kept clean and without product, the nail plate should reattach itself in time and then artificial nails may be reapplied. A pharmacist should be able to suggest what will keep under the nail clean.
- A white area under the nail plate could also be nail separation that has allowed in a bacteria or fungus. This must always be referred to a GP and the products removed.
- A further possibility could be a reaction to the products, either as an allergy or too much dehydration or as a result of a badly fitting tip putting too much stress on the nail plate.

In all cases the products must be removed.

Skin reaction

- If there is any **irritation** of the skin, such as itching, swelling, redness or a rash anywhere on the body but especially on the hands, fingers or face, the products must be removed immediately.

- If this is done as soon as any slight reaction is noticed the condition will stop. (It is very rare, but possible, that a severe reaction occurs suddenly without a warning.) The reaction will stop as soon as the irritant is removed. If acted upon quickly, the irritation will be mild and clear up quickly. If it does not stop within 24 hours or gets worse or if the reaction is more severe, then the client should visit a GP as soon as possible. This is an allergic reaction to one or more of the products or their ingredients. (If the reaction does not stop after all products have been removed, it is possible that it occurred as a result of another allergen that has nothing to do with the nails.) If the client wants to wear artificial nails after this (and many do) it is possible to slowly reintroduce some products by way of a patch test or a test nail to see what product or products must be avoided.
- If a technician does not act responsibly and follow these guidelines, the condition may become serious and could result in permanent damage to the client's skin or nails. This could result in litigation where the technician is held responsible if the correct advice was not given and the correct procedure was not followed. Public and product liability insurance will not cover a technician who has not acted in a professional manner and followed accepted industry guidelines.

The maintenance treatment

Once this stage has been completed and any points noted on the record card, the maintenance treatment can begin. The equipment required is exactly the same as for the first application. Any artificial nails that are missing will need to have a tip replaced in the same way as previously described.

Procedure for infills (one hand at a time for liquid and powder or a fibre system and two hands for a UV-cured system):

1 Have the desk prepared and all tools, equipment and products ready plus the record card completed with notes from the consultation at the start of the appointment.
2 Sanitize hands.
3 Sanitize and dehydrate nails with appropriate product on a nail wipe or cotton wool by wiping the whole nail from the tip towards the nail fold.
4 With cuticle tool, remove any cuticle that is on the newly grown nail.
5 Using a 240 grit file, gently blend the edge of the overlay in Zone 3. This will also remove the shine. If there is any lifting of the overlay in this area it will need to be buffed away, carefully and without overbuffing the nail plate. This can sometimes be time-consuming as more overlay can lift as it is being thinned out. There is no real safe short cut to this process. Many technicians use some short cuts such as nipping with cuticle nippers (this can lift away overlay that is

bonded to the nail and take some nail plate with it) or getting adhesive to run under lifting area (this could trap any bacteria that may be present) or using a solvent in the expectation that it will deal with any bacteria or fungus (the solvent can get trapped and the area will still be unattached).

6 The shine should be removed from the whole nail surface.

7 Remove the dust with the dehydrator, taking care to clean around the side walls and nail fold, and apply primer if required.

8 Apply a thin layer of the product (liquid and powder, UV gel or resin) in Zone 3 as in the original application and blend it to the rest of the nail.

9 With a 240 grit file, shape the overlay as in the first application, checking from all angles that the structure of curves is right.

10 Refine surface with white block

11 Finish with a three-way buffer or high-gloss sealant (after removing all traces of dust).

12 Apply oil.

Procedure for a rebalance:

1 Follow steps 1–4 as above

5 Shorten the length of the nail to the length and shape that was originally agreed.

6 Thin out the whole overlay, removing the apex so that the remaining overlay is a thin and even coating. Ensure that the tip of the free edge is very thin as, by shortening the length, the free edge will be thicker than the original tip and this will need thinning. (As the overlay is old, a harsher **abrasive** may be used to speed up the process, but care must be taken that the exposed natural nail is not buffed and the overlay is not buffed down to the nail plate by mistake.)

7 Clean nails with the dehydrator to remove all the dust and prepare the exposed nail. Prime if required.

8 Apply a new overlay in exactly the same way as the original overlay was applied. (If it is a fibre system and the original fibre had not been disturbed, it is not necessary to apply the fibre to the whole nail as it will get too thick as time goes on. A small piece of fibre placed in Zone 3 will be sufficient.)

9 Shape, refine and bring to a high shine as usual.

SELF-ASSESSMENT SKILLS

Opportunities to learn

- It is at the maintenance stage that the trainee technician can learn a great deal. Obviously teaching and coaching by a good trainer is essential but the beginner can continue to improve every time a client is seen without the trainer present. This can be done by self-assessment. A dedicated technician will always assess their work as there is always room for improvement but this will probably be done in an informal and basically unstructured way.

- Many professional and dedicated technicians enter competitions to help them improve their standards. A good person to assess 'nails' is an experienced technician who will study them from an objective view point. At the end of any competition the judges are available for a 'critique' and the best technicians will take this opportunity happily. They do not go to 'argue about the score' but they go to find out what an objective opinion about their nails is. They may agree or they may disagree but there is a good chance that a good and objective judge may see something that the technician has missed, usually because they are looking too hard!
- Good technicians will also go to many workshops and seminars held by various companies and trainers. This is because they may learn something new that will improve their skills or an assessment on their performance may be available that may or may not be useful.
- Beginners need to develop many skills and they also need to develop or improve an 'eye' for balance and symmetry. A beginner should never miss an opportunity to do this and every client provides an ideal opportunity until such time as competitions can be entered and workshops and seminars attended.

A self-assessment programme

The following is a suggestion of how a trainee or beginner (or even an experienced technician dedicated to improvement) can carry out an effective self-assessment. The self-assessment should be used in conjunction with a record card, and it assumes that the first application is as good as the technician is able to achieve at the time.

First maintenance

- Describe each section of each nail (*Observation*):
  a. Shape on looking down onto nail:
  b. Shape from sides:
  c. Shape of barrel:
  d. Smile line:
  e. Clarity of overlay:
  f. Zone 3:
  g. General:
- Client's responses (*Questioning*):
  a. How did the nails break? (If appropriate!)
  b. How have you managed with them?
  c. Have you followed all homecare advice?
  d. If not, what has been missed?
  e. Do you like the length and shape?
  f. Have they caused any problem?
- Correction of any present problems (*Diagnosis and treatment*):
  a. Shape:
  b. Breakages:

c. Clarity of product:

d. Lifting:

e. Chipping:

f. Allergic reaction or infections:

- Finished nails (this section does not need recording, just careful observation):

    a. Free edge shape – each nail and in comparison with each other:

    b. Upper arch – each nail and in comparison with each other:

    c. Lower arch – ditto:

    d. 'C' curve – ditto:

    e. Smile line – ditto:

    f. Clarity – ditto:

    g. Free margin – each nail.

Second maintenance

As with the record of first maintenance, look at and ask all the same points. Compare results and determine if problems have been solved and results improved. If this is not the case, make a note of what is not right as before and complete a full self-assessment.

NAIL DISEASES AND DISORDERS

There can be a great deal of confusion among technicians about the various nail diseases and disorders that may be seen on clients' fingers. Educators and information from various companies has been at best confusing, and at worst, contradictory. Even one of the most popular textbooks on the subject of nail technology contradicts itself in different chapters! How can technicians who want to do the right thing know what is the right thing to do?

There is one common and one not so common condition that technicians are likely to see during their career and available information can be confusing.

Green nails

This condition is likely to be seen by most technicians at some point but, hopefully, not too often. It is usually seen during maintenance visits or may come with a new client who has been going to another technician.

What type of 'green nails'?

- At this stage it is important to describe exactly what type of 'green nails' we are dealing with. Is there a yellow/green stain on top of the nail plate but under an artificial overlay of any description? This stain is always associated with an area where the overlay has lifted from the nail plate, usually in the cuticle or side wall area and sometimes on the free edge of the natural nail plate. This type of green nail is not connected with any discolouration *under* the natural nail plate on the nail bed, nor is it connected with a green nail plate that has never had an artificial nail applied to it.

- The differentiation between these various conditions is essential and is often where the confusion lies. An important aspect of the nail technician's knowledge and practice is to recognize skin and nail conditions but never to diagnose them. Technicians are not medically trained and dermatologists would have difficulty diagnosing genuine medical conditions without carrying out tests.

- Confusion with these conditions seems to always involve the words 'bacterial', 'fungal', **'mould'** and **'yeast'**. The next confusion is whether a technician should treat the condition, send the client to a doctor, apply nails, not apply nails, take nails off, leave alone to go away.

- This condition, as described, will always be associated with a lifting artificial nail overlay. (If the discoloration is trapped under the overlay, this will usually mean that the client, or technician, has reattached the overlay by getting nail adhesive to seep under.) A lifted overlay provides an ideal environment for a certain type of bacteria to find a home, settle down and multiply! The environment is warm and lovely and moist with the water that has seeped in. It also has very little oxygen and does not get disturbed. As the first little bacterium starts to multiply it has yellow 'metabolic byproduct' but as more and more bacteria are created, the yellow colour darkens to green and, if left alone, it will eventually appear black. The nail plate can start to become soft and the nail bed can become tender as the bacteria colony breaks the nail plate down and eventually destroys it.

- A good technician will make sure that clients are seen at regular and appropriate intervals. New clients should be seen no more than 2 weeks apart until the technician and client know exactly what to expect from artificial nails. The best technicians will sometimes experience a little lifting on clients' nails, especially new clients. If rebooking and client education is carried out properly then any sign of trouble will be detected before it becomes a major problem.

Treating a bacterial infection

- If a client returns for a maintenance visit and there is a patch of yellow under a corner of the overlay, there is the beginning of a bacterial infection. It should never be any more than a pale yellowy-green if the client has returned for the correct appointment or understands that any change in the appearance of the nails needs an immediate return visit. The experienced technician can treat this condition, as it is mild and not necessarily infectious.

- **The artificial nail must be removed.** If the natural nail is hard, very gently buff with a few strokes of a fine grit file. This may remove the colour but do not buff any more if the colour remains (it is safest to discard or disinfect the file).

If the nail feels soft where the stain is, do not replace the artificial nail for a few weeks. After gentle buffing dehydrate the nail plate with an alcohol-based dehydrator. This will remove the bacteria and take away the environment it needs to survive. A new artificial nail can now be applied. The yellow colour will probably remain slightly and grow up with the nail plate as it is a stain only. If the stain changes in shape or colour, the bacteria is still active and the process was not carried out effectively and must be repeated more thoroughly.

- Some technicians recommend that the stain is removed by using a mild bleaching agent. As these are water-based it is better to leave the stain to grow out as soaking the nail plate in water and another chemical may cause a further problem with lifting and soft nail plates as the water is trapped under the overlay.
- This treatment should not be carried out if the technician is not totally confident that the cause of the problem is as described. Nor should it be carried out if the infection has progressed further than a pale green colour or the nail plate is very soft. If this happens, the artificial nail should be removed in a tip remover and not replaced. If the condition continues to spread or does not start improving in a few days, the client should go to their doctor.
- Other types of bacterial, fungal or yeast infections are very rare on the fingernails. They are more common on the toenails as the toes spend a lot of their life in the warm, moist condition of a shoe. They are possible to have on a fingernail and, depending on the type, can affect the nail plate, the nail bed and the soft tissue surrounding the nail. A technician must *never* diagnose any of these conditions and the golden rule is: 'When in any doubt, don't.' It is only a dermatologist who has carried out tests that can accurately diagnose a genuine infection and such infections are very rare. They also take a long time to clear once diagnosis has been made.

White spots on the nails

The second condition that a technician may see and is likely to be confused about is a fungal infection that creates white spots on the nails. It is more common on the toenails but can affect fingernails.

- I am sure every technician has had the client with a couple of white spots on their nails who says, 'I know this is a lack of calcium'. I hope every technician has also answered that it is very unlikely that it is a lack of calcium. It is most likely that they are little patches caused by trauma to the nail plate. The whiteness is caused by the nail plate layers slightly parting. If any client suffers from a lack in an essential mineral like calcium or zinc there are likely to be other symptoms and the last of their worries would be spotty nails!

- It is possible, however, to confuse this very common condition with a more serious (but rare) fungal infection. If the nail has white spots or areas that appear soft and chalky on the surface of the nail, it is possible that the client has a fungal infection called leukonychia mycotica, and this can be easily spread by buffing. This condition does not always appear on every nail and can run along a ridge rather than be a spot.
- Like all conditions, the technician must not diagnose but should recommend that their client should see a doctor without scaring the client. In the greater scheme of things, this infection is not serious but it is contagious and can spread to other nails, the technician and other clients. It is also not very pleasant for the client who has gone to a technician to improve the appearance of their nails. They want nice nails not white crumbly ones (or green ones), and it should be the expertise of the technician who points them in the right direction to try to achieve their aim.

SUMMARY

This chapter has demonstrated the value of a regular maintenance programme for the health of a client's hands, and outlined how the technician should approach some of the more common diseases and disorders that may be encountered in a client. 'Maintenance' of the technician's expanding skill base is no less important, as the self-assessment exercises make very clear.

CHAPTER 10

Nail Art, Basic and Advanced

INTRODUCTION

Nail art is a very important part of the technician's skill. Just painting colour on nails is nail art! Many technicians do not master this art and assume that they can do it naturally. Not true! It takes practise and a very good eye for detail, as this chapter shows, demonstrating both basic and advanced airbrushing techniques.

The nail art skill becomes more advanced when a 'French manicure' is applied, as this is actually two colours painted very accurately. The skill becomes even more advanced when other colours and actual designs become involved. A technician does not need to be a great artist in order to create quite stunning and very commercially acceptable designs. A natural artist will obviously find this aspect of the work easy but a 'struggling' artist can generate just as much income with some easy short cuts.

There are many products available on the market today that, with a few guidelines and hints, can create stunning 'masterpieces' at minimal cost and effort. The real effort is practising! This cannot be skipped. Nail art is visual and there are relatively few basic techniques that, using readily available products, can be demonstrated in a few step-by-step pictures. Every newcomer to nail art has found that, with the right direction and range of products, a few ideas will lead on to many, many more. Technicians should aim to create their own masterpieces; it is very difficult to copy another person's work but it is easy to be inspired by ideas.

THE BASIC TECHNIQUES

All the basic techniques are easy! All they need is some ideas, a bit of imagination and the right equipment and products.

Nail paints

These are different from nail varnishes. They are usually water-based acrylic artists' paint as this type of paint gives a very dense colour, can be mixed and is easier to use for fine detail. There are lots of effects that can be achieved with paints, a selection of nail art brushes and a 'marbling tool'.

Nails need to be painted with a base colour that will be part of or enhance the finished design. This is usually a nail varnish that should be touch dry before painting any designs:

- Very simple but effective designs can be achieved by placing *dots of colour*. Either a very small round brush or a 'marbling tool' can apply the dots. Care needs to be taken on the size and regularity of the dots as this can spoil a good design.

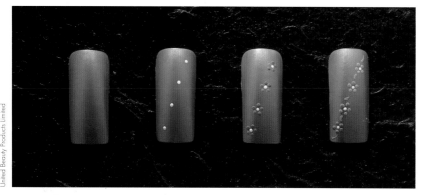

Daisy Chain
1 Paint nail with base colour and wait until touch dry
2 Apply line of dots in colour chosen to be centre of flowers
3 Apply dots in second colour to surround each centre
4 Join up flowers with green leaves

- A very long, thin brush dipped in paint can achieve *fine stripes* and can create quite sophisticated designs.
- *Abstract patterns or marbling* can look good with a good choice of colour combinations. Either flicking colour from side to side with a fine brush or placing spots of colour on the nail and mixing them together with the 'marbling tool' achieves this.
- Those who are not so good at hand painting designs can use *stencils*. The types that are readily available have a sticky back to keep them in place. These are applied to a *dry* nail and painted over. When the nail paint is completely dry they are removed, leaving the chosen design behind.

Selection of freehand nail art brushes

Nail art stencils

| 1 | 2 | 3 | 4 | 5 |

Frosty the Snowman
1 Apply deep blue varnish
2 Paint an uneven purple colour near to cuticle
3 With white nail art paint, cover free edge of nail and paint shape of snowman (if the paint is applied thickly, it will dry and crack to give the effect of snow on the ground). Draw a couple of branches beside the snowman
4 Using black paint, draw details on snowman, footprints in snow and tree
5 Apply thin coat of fine holographic glitter to represent snow

- Pictures of all sorts can be painted on a nail with a steady hand, a good imagination or an easy picture to copy. (Most nail artists keep loads of pictures to copy on to a nail or just to give them inspiration to create an original design.)

This type of paint is water-based and any mistakes can be easily removed with a wet nail wipe or a cotton bud to remove a small part.

Like all nail art, sealing the design is very important and, when the paint is dry, a *sealer or topcoat* must be applied to fix the paint and also bring out the colour. The manufacturer's recommended sealer should be used as some topcoats may react to the paints. Clients should be advised to re-seal the nails every couple of days to keep them fresh looking and avoid any chips.

Designs using a variety of paint techniques

Foils

Another very easy technique uses various designs of foil that is supplied on a roll. This is almost instant nail art as some foils have designs on them and just need applying to a painted nail.

A foil nail art kit

- Nails should be painted before using foils. They can be painted with a base coat but it is worth spending the extra time to paint a colour, as this will enhance the effect.
- Foils are supplied with a special adhesive that should be painted on the nail in a very thin coat. The adhesive is usually white and needs to turn clear before the foil is applied; this takes a very short time. The foil is then applied to the tacky adhesive, pattern side uppermost, gently pressed on the nail with either a finger or a cotton bud and the backing pulled off leaving the foil behind. It is not necessary to cut any foil from the roll, as it will only stick to where the adhesive is.

1   2   3   4   5

Party popper
1 Apply patches of foil adhesive to nail, allow to become clear and press gold foil on to nail
2 Repeat with green foil, placing adhesive in some of the spaces between gold foil
3 Fill all spaces with blue then red foil
4 Seal foil with correct sealer and apply a coat of glitter polish
5 Add some metal shapes to wet polish and seal with several coats of sealer

- This is an amazingly quick process with spectacular results. As the foil only sticks to where the adhesive has been applied, patterns or pictures can be drawn with the adhesive. The foil needs a special sealer, as most topcoats will destroy the delicate layer. Several layers of sealer are also needed, as with all nail art, to keep it intact.

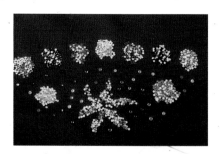

Designs using a variety of foiling techniques

Selection of the various types of polish secures

Polish secures

As the name suggests, this technique requires polish to secure the design. Many different products are available for this easy technique. They are all small stones or shapes with a flat back and this is the only technique that needs wet nail varnish!

- After the base colour has been applied (or other designs) a topcoat or sealer must be painted. While this is still wet, the 'secures' can be placed on it. The easiest way to pick up 'secures' is with a wet orange stick or with a small piece of 'Blu Tac' on the end of an orange stick. The 'Blu Tac' can be shaped into a point to make picking up the tiny shapes easier.
- When all the shapes have been placed, the whole nail needs sealing with several thick coats of sealer or topcoat.

Designs showing a variety of ways that polish secures can be used

Glitter dusts

A glitter dust nail art kit

Glitter polishes and glitter dusts are a very versatile range of products to have to create or enhance nail art. Obviously, glitter can be applied to the whole nail, but it can also be used to make patterns or designs; a well-placed highlight on a painted or airbrushed design can make a simple piece of nail art spectacular.

- Glitter polishes can be painted straight from the bottle with either the brush supplied or a fine nail art brush. Glitter dusts can be used to create more specific designs by picking up the dust with a brush dipped in sealer, as this will give an effect that is denser than glitter polish. The dust will also stick to wet sealer, so the tip of a nail dipped into the pot will collect the dust on the tip only or where the sealer is wet.

Designs using glitter dust

- Like all nail art, the glitter dusts need sealing. The sealer needs to be painted on thickly and gently to avoid moving the dust.

Transfers and tapes

Many transfers are available to apply to nails. These are ready-made nail art and can be very effective. They are either the type that need to be soaked off their backing with water (place a few

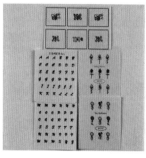
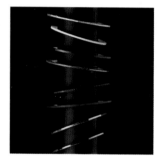
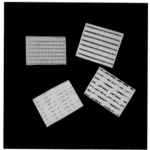

Some of the tapes and stencils available

1   2   3   4

Gold stripe
1 Apply three diagonal stripes of complementary colours to the nail
2 Blend colours together with brush
3 Apply strips of gold tape horizontally across nail and trim to size
4 Apply sealer, paying special attention to edges of foil

drops onto the backing paper to soak through and then the transfer slides off) or they peel off their backing and stick straight on to the nail.

Tapes are also available in many plain colours and patterns. They have a sticky back and must be placed on the nail and then trimmed with a small pair of very sharp scissors.

Designs using tapes and stencils

Nail jewellry

Many different types of nail jewellry are now available.

- Some of the designs are applied to the nail as a 'polish secure', that is to stick to wet varnish. These can only be very light and small. Larger designs can be applied to the nail with nail glue. Both of these are reusable as they can be removed with nail varnish remover.
- Other types of nail jewellry involve making a small hole in the free edge of the nail. This can be done with ease using a specially made tool that has a very sharp but tiny drill. There is no problem at all piercing an artificial nail but care must be taken when piercing a natural nail:
  - A natural nail should be strengthened with a coating of resin used in a fibre system.
  - The free edge must be long enough to provide a space for the hole without being too close to the hyponychium. If the hole is made on a nail that is too short the seal at the hyponychium could be damaged.
- There are two types of jewellry that require a pierced nail. One has a post that is put through the hole and secured with a tiny nut on the underside. The piercing tool has both the drill and the socket to tighten the nut. The other type has a clasp or ring that is attached to the nail through the hole. Usually the first type sits on top of the nail plate and the second hangs from the edge.

    To pierce the nail:

    1 Make sure there is sufficient free edge to safely pierce.
    2 Turn the finger over so that the underside of the nail is visible and the nail and finger are resting on a soft surface, for example, a piece of cork or several layers of tissues.
    3 Place the tip of the drill on the nail that is not too near the edge but also in the right place for the jewellry to fit on the nail (not too far away from the free edge for a pendant or ring).
    4 Gently turn the drill until a neat hole is made; withdraw the drill by turning in the opposite direction.
    5 Turn the finger over and smooth the surface of the nail with a white block.
    6 Apply the nail jewellry
    7 If a pendant has been applied, advise the client to remove it while dressing, doing housework, washing hair, etc., as it is possible to catch it and split the nail.

These have been some basic instructions for starting off in the realms of nail art. All the various techniques can be mixed and matched. Foil can be mixed with polish secures, paint mixed with glitter. The possibilities are endless and the only limit is imagination.

Nail piercing tool and decorated nail with pendant

1	2	3	4

United Beauty Products Limited

Using texture
1 Apply base colour to nail and allow to dry
2 Paint an uneven layer of nail art paint in complementary colour
3 While paint is still wet, take a tissue and press into paint to create an uneven texture
4 Seal and apply thin coat of glitter polish

MORE ADVANCED TECHNIQUES

Airbrushing

A process that is becoming very popular among technicians and their clients is airbrushing. Unlike basic nail art, this requires relatively costly equipment and, more importantly, plenty of investment in time for practise. Like artificial nail skills, it tends to look very easy in the hands of an expert but in reality takes a fair bit of skill.

- In the US, airbrushing is rapidly overtaking traditional nail polishing and, believe it or not, some salons no longer offer **nail polish** as a free service! And of course, the more services your salon offers, the more valuable you are to your clientele! Airbrushing is now one of the fastest-growing nail services that can not only create the most amazing designs but can take the place of traditional nail painting as colour is applied to the nails in such a short space of time.
- Airbrushed artwork is a professional skill, which requires specialized techniques and methods of application. There are many products available on the market, and time should be taken in finding the right package of equipment. Training courses are essential for this skill as nothing can take the place of practical instruction.

Equipment

This section is designed to give technicians some idea of what the skill entails and some ideas on airbrushing designs, as well as giving an idea on how the essential equipment works.

The electrical compressor: The technique needs an electrical compressor that provides the air. These are available in many different shapes, sizes and prices. In essence, there are two main types: the compressor that produces air on demand and that which stores compressed air in a tank that is refilled as the air

Gina Wallace

Selection of designs using hand painting techniques

United Beauty Products Limited

Two types of compressors
The smaller of the two is the type that supplies air on demand. The gauge on the top shows the pressure of air being provided by the machine. The large compressor is one that manufactures compressed air and stores it in a tank. The two gauges on the front show the pressure of air being provided and the pressure of air stored in the tank. Both machines have glass moisture traps that hold water that can collect due to condensation. The picture also shows a four-way adaptor that allows up to four air brushes to be used on one machine.

HEALTH AND SAFETY
Check your psi level every time
you start to use the compressor

is used. The air is dispensed under pressure and is therefore potentially dangerous. Care must be taken at all times but specifically concerning two points:

1 Follow all manufacturers' instructions with regard to *maintenance*. If none are provided the manufacturer must be asked what the procedures are. The equipment should also be serviced once a year: a faulty compressor can be dangerous.

2 The *pressure of the air being dispensed* should be around 30 psi (pounds per square inch) and never more than 35 psi. Every compressor should have a psi gauge and regulator to set this level. A pressure of more than 40 psi can push paint (or any other liquid in the airbrush) into the pores of the skin and possibly into the blood stream.

The first option tends to be cheaper, smaller and lighter and is ideal for mobile technicians or salons where airbrushing demands are minimal. The difficulty with this type is that the compressor can only be used for fairly short time limits before it gets too hot and the amount of air produced is limited. The storage type of compressor is more suited for use in the salon as it can be used continuously and can often provide air for more than one technician at a time. However, this type is heavier and difficult to move around and is more costly.

There is a certain amount of maintenance required for most compressors, such as draining the tanks and moisture traps and making sure oil levels are right. The least amount of maintenance is obviously better for the user.

The airbrush: The crucial part of the equipment needed is the airbrush itself. This is where the air created by the compressor is mixed with the paint and a fine mist of colour is dispensed on to the nail. There are several different types of airbrush but the practicalities of dispensing the colour are the same for all.

• On the front of the airbrush is a very fine *nozzle in a cone shape*. A pointed needle fits into this and when the needle is furthest forward the nozzle is blocked but as the needle is pulled back more and more air and paint can escape. It is the movement of this needle that regulates the flow of paint from a shut position to a small mist of paint to the maximum flow. The trigger that also regulates the flow of air moves the needle.

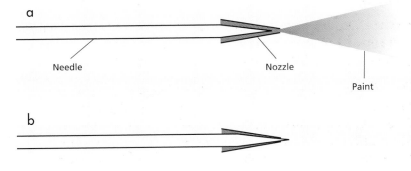

a

Needle   Nozzle

Paint

b

Flow of paint in airbrush
a Needle back in nozzle leaving
   nozzle open to allow paint
   through
b Needle in nozzle sealing nozzle

- The air, supplied by a compressor, is fed into the airbrush by a *hose* that is usually attached under the airbrush. The trigger is sprung and, when depressed, opens a valve to allow the air in and out through the nozzle.

Gravity-fed air brush
The funnel on the top is where the paint is placed. The air hose is attached to the valve at the bottom and the regulator can be seen at the back of the airbrush. This piece of equipment is a dual-action airbrush and it can be seen that the trigger, on the top, can be depressed and also pulled back.

Gravity-fed and bottle-fed paint: The paint is dispensed into the airbrush by one of two methods, depending on the type of equipment:

1 *Gravity-fed*. These airbrushes have a hole in the top or a funnel on the side where small quantities of paint are placed as required. Flushing the old colour through and adding another to the funnel change colours.
2 *Bottle-fed*. On some airbrushes there is an attachment on the side that fits a specific bottle that is filled with paint colour. Colour changing, after flushing, is by changing the bottle.

The type used is dependent on the preference of the artist and other factors such as cost, availability, and so on.

Single-action or dual-action operation: The other decision a new artist must decide is the type of operation preferred:

Single-action bottle-fed air brush
The bottle containing the paint is attached to the side and the regulator is clearly seen on the back. As before, the air hose is connected to the valve at the bottom and the air controlled by the trigger on the top

1 *Single action*. The trigger on this type of airbrush can only be pushed down to release the air. The regulation of the amount of paint being dispensed (that is, how far the needle is pulled back from the nozzle to open it up) is set. The needle is set at the beginning of the spraying session to the level that is appropriate for the application. It can be opened up to allow efficient cleaning but otherwise remains the same. This type of airbrush is good for beginners as the spraying techniques and designs can be concentrated on more. However, most airbrushes of this type need two hands; one to press the trigger, the other to change the regulator and some artists are not keen on this.
2 *Dual action*. The trigger on these airbrushes can be depressed for air and pulled back to move the needle and therefore regulate the paint. The combination of air to paint regulation is infinitely variable and many artists prefer to have this option. Co-ordination is essential for this operation, and takes a bit more practise.
3 *Combination*. Some equipment can be used as either of the above. The difference in these is that not only do they have a dual-action trigger, but they also have a regulator that can set the position of the needle. This is a good option, especially for beginners. The needle can be set in a position that does not allow too much paint out so thought does not have to be given to regulation by the trigger. When the artist is more skilful and confident the regulator can be left alone and the air to paint ratio can be controlled by the dual-action trigger (and a very delicate finger movement).

Paint: The paint used in airbrushes for the purpose of nail art is usually water-based acrylic artists' paint that is the consistency of milk. Any thicker and it will keep blocking the equipment; any thinner and coverage will be a problem. Most of the paints available on the market are easily washed off skin with water. Therefore paint that is sprayed over the nail is sealed with a clear topcoat, like nail varnish, and the paint on the skin can be washed off when the sealer is dry. Some paints need to be removed from the skin with a nail varnish remover.

Cleaning the airbrush: Cleaning the airbrush is *the most essential stage* for efficient and correct working. It is a stage that so many try to short cut and wonder why the airbrush will not work. The paint is air-dried and little flakes of it remain in the airbrush if cleaning is not thorough. These flakes are then dislodged during use and block the nozzle. Flushing through between colours takes a very short time but, more importantly, thorough cleaning after use must be carried out. Manufacturers should supply cleaning instructions and these should be followed to the letter. Most 'broken' airbrushes are caused by:

1 Short-cut cleaning so they are blocked
2 Short-cut cleaning so needles are removed and poked into nozzles to remove blockages. This results in bent and damaged needles and split nozzles!

For beginners to airbrushing, practise and discovery are the keys to good work and enthusiasm. Every beginner should discover their own effects and colour mixes. It is very satisfying!

Techniques of layering colour

Before this discovery starts there are a few concepts regarding colour that need to be understood. Airbrushing is all about layering colour. Layering one colour on top of another will produce a different colour. This is an effect that will often be required. However, there will also be as many (if not more) occasions when the uppermost colour needs to be a true colour (as with stencil work). In order to achieve this the lower colour must be covered up to produce a colour-free area. This is achieved by spraying white in the area to mask the lower colour. The top colour can then be added over the white.

Techniques of airbrushing

We shall now look at the basic techniques in airbrushing. This is just the beginning; experimentation and practise (and time) are what produces a skilled artist.

The working area: The first step is to collect all the necessary equipment together and prepare a working area:

• Compressor
• Air hose

HEALTH AND SAFETY
Never think you have finished a day's painting until you have cleaned the airbrush

- Airbrush
- Cleaning brush
- Cleaning fluid
- Cup of water
- Empty paint bottle filled with water
- Cleaning unit to spray unused paint and cleaner into (in the absence of a specifically designed unit, a paper cup with disposable towels in it will suffice or, even better, a small 'Pringles' tube with disposable towels in it and a hole made in the plastic lid)
- Plenty of waterproof protection on desk
- Paper towels
- Base coat
- Top coat/sealer
- Selection of airbrush paints
- Plastic tips
- 'Blu Tac'
- Finger rest (optional)
- Stencils.

Loading and cleaning: Next, basecoat plenty of tips ready to practise airbrushing (the paint will not adhere to a plain tip). Practising loading the airbrush with colour and cleaning it out is very important and manufacturers' instructions should be followed. As a basic guideline the following steps can be taken:

1 Add your chosen colour paint to a clean airbrush.
2 The paint needs to be 'blasted' through to get it to the nozzle quickly. The method of doing this will depend on the type of airbrush being used. The nozzle needs to be opened to its maximum to let as much paint through as possible and the air also needs to be at maximum strength. This should get the paint to the nozzle quickly. Spray the airbrush onto a disposable towel until the colour appears and then adjust the level of paint spray until there is a fine mist. (Paint should not be seen coming out of the airbrush. If the spray can be seen the level of paint is too high – that is, the nozzle is open too far.)
3 With the colour loaded, practise spraying a fine straight line of dense colour on the towel by holding the airbrush close to the surface. Then practise spraying a thicker, less dense line by holding the airbrush a bit further away. Adjust the amount of paint mixing with the air. Try this several times until you are aware of how the control of air and the control of paint, together with the distance of the airbrush is away from the surface, affects the results. Far better results are achieved if the colour is built up with several layers rather than trying to create an intense colour immediately.

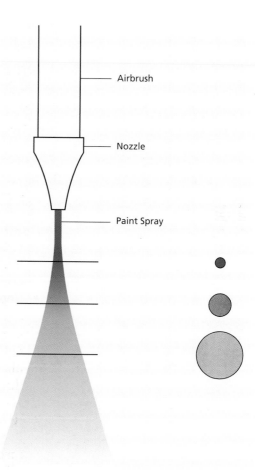

Distance management of airbrush

4 Now practise cleaning in between colours. This should be a very quick process (major cleaning must take place at the end of the session). Spray all the remaining paint into your cup. Add clean water to the airbrush and spray it into your cup. Repeat this a few times until all paint is flushed through. It may be necessary to flush through some of the recommended cleaning fluid. Dip your cleaning brush in water and clean the end of the nozzle to remove any flakes of dried paint that have collected there.

5 Once all the paint has been cleaned away, a new colour can be added.

6 At the end of the session, a thorough clean must be carried out. Manufacturers' instructions for this should be followed, as each different airbrush has different removable parts. Never leave your airbrush without this thorough cleaning as it can make the equipment unusable.

Gradient blends:

- Choose three complementary colours, and have the bottles ready.
- Place at least four basecoated tips on a towel, using 'Blu Tac' to secure them.

Diagonal   Horizontal   Vertical   Mixed

Gradient blends

- Get the flow of paint correct by spraying on the towel and then carry the spray across a corner of one of the tips to create a diagonal stripe. Do not spray too close to the tip. Keep spraying across the corner until the colour intensity is dense in the corner but decreasing in density as it goes closer to the centre of the tip. Repeat this on the next tip as a horizontal line, then on the next as a vertical. Finally, try to create small patches of colour on the fourth tip.
- Repeat this on other tips until you achieve lines of colour that are denser on the outer edge than in the centre.
- Clean out the paint and load the next colour.
- Spray a line of the new colour close to the first one, but making the dense colour in the centre of the line. Where the thinner colour overlays the first colour there should be another colour created where the two colours mix.
- Repeat for all other tips.
- Repeat process with the third colour until you have tips with three colours blended on them in various ways.

  Note: The stripes should not have any shape edges. The area between each colour should be soft and another colour from the two on either side.

This technique is often used as a base for many designs in airbrushing, hand painting and other nail art techniques. It is the basis of airbrushing and is worth spending time to master.

Stencils: Stencils are precut shapes in a thin plastic sheet. They can be abstract shapes or specific shapes. The stencil can have shapes cut into the plastic forming holes that the paint is sprayed through, or shapes cut out of the side of the plastic.

- There are many ways a stencil can be used. It is not just a case of spraying a blast of paint through a hole. First the stencil must be held properly. A nail curves in two directions and the stencil must be held in such a way that allows for these curves. It must also be held so that you can see what you are doing.

- The stencil must be held from the top, away from you so you are not covering your work (see airbrushing step-by-step sequence). Choose the shape of image you want to use; if you are right-handed, you will need to use your left hand (as your right is holding the airbrush); hold your forefinger and middle finger together, then bring your ring finger and thumb together; it is with these fingers that you will need to hold the stencil. Put your ring and middle fingers on one side of the chosen image and your ring finger and thumb on the other side and bring the two sides together. This will make the stencil bend slightly, creating a curve that will sit closely on the nail. Try this a few times until you feel reasonably comfortable holding a stencil.

- Have plenty of basecoated tips ready. It is easier if you now use a finger rest and secure the tip onto it. Try holding a stencil on a nail and spraying a colour. See how you get on and keep trying until you can control both the stencil and the airbrush and get reasonable results. Now you are ready to try some stencil techniques:

  - **Overlap**. Choose a shape from the centre of the stencil (not the edge) and hold it closely on the nail. Spray. With a different colour, place the same shape on the stencil against the first colour and slightly overlapping and spray. *Or* choose a shape from the edge of the stencil and repeat the same process.

  - **Soft blow**. Hold an image very slightly above the nail and gently spray. The shape produced should have soft edges.

  - **Hard blow**. Hold the same image closely on the nail and spray with several layers to build up the intensity of colour. This should produce a strong colour with sharp edges.

  - **Double blow**. This is where two colours are used in the one image or shape. The stencil needs to be replaced in exactly the same place to apply the second colour.

  - **Triple blow**. The same principle as above with three colours.

  - **Graduation**. This is a similar principle as the blended colours but includes the use of a stencil. The image or shape is moved slightly and another colour added.

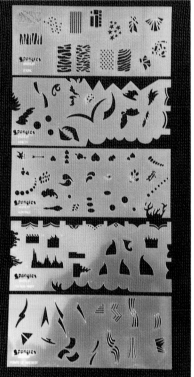

Examples of stencils

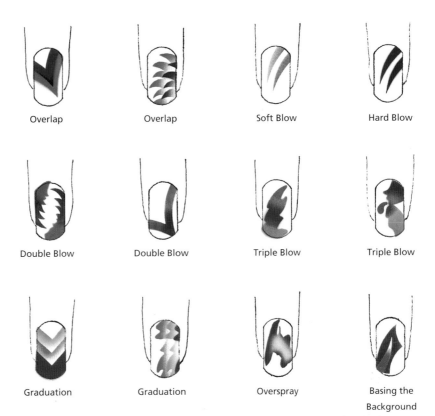

Overlap	Overlap	Soft Blow	Hard Blow
Double Blow	Double Blow	Triple Blow	Triple Blow
Graduation	Graduation	Overspray	Basing the Background

More gradient blends

- **Overspray**. If an image is chosen from the centre of the stencil and the paint is concentrated around the edges, it will produce an image that is pale in the centre and more intense at the edges.
- **Basing the background**. This is one of the most important techniques and basic concepts in airbrushing. It is needed if a colour is going to be sprayed over another colour. If this is done without basing the first colour, the two will mix to create a third-colour variation. If the second colour needs to be true this technique must be used. Choose the image for the second colour and place closely on the nail. Spray white until the base colour is covered. Change to the second colour and place the stencil in exactly the same place as before and spray.

Other accessories: Other accessories can be used to create wonderful effects.

- As an alternative to ready-made stencils, there is a product called Frisket Film that is a sticky-backed plastic that can be used as a mask. This can be cut into any shape with a sharp scalpel and placed onto a nail that has a base colour. Colours can sprayed over the whole nail and then the film removed. Where the film covered the nail the base colour will show through. (Striping tape can be used for this. Several strips laid close together and then colours blended over the top look very effective when the tape is removed.)

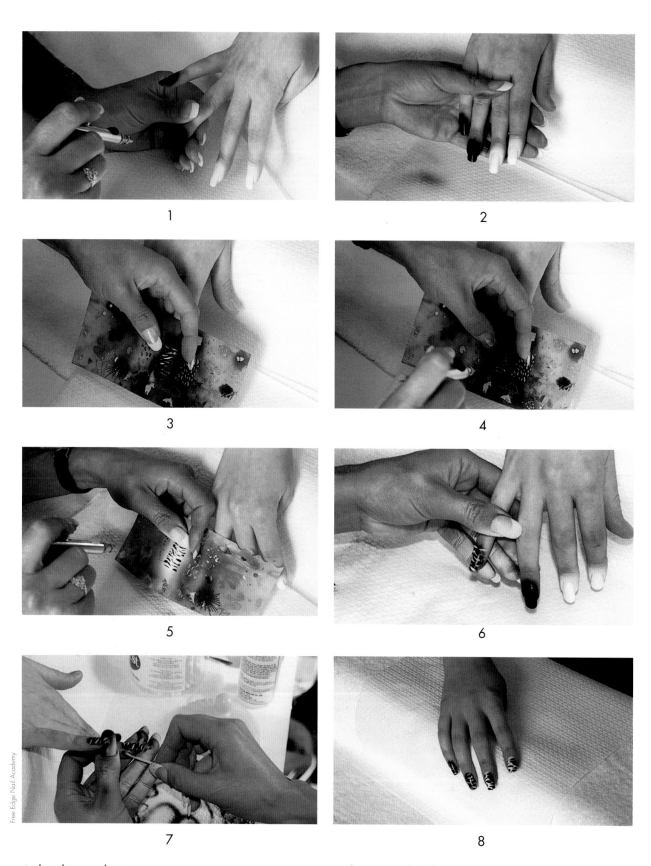

1

2

3

4

5

6

7

8

Airbrushing technique
1 Spray nails with base colour
2 Nails sprayed
3–5 Holding and placement of stencils

6 The sprayed nail
7 Once a top coat has been applied to seal the design you should clean up the nail
8 The completed nails

Free Edge Nail Academy

- Another useful accessory is lace. Apply a base colour to the nail. Hold a piece of lace on the nail and base it with white; than spray a second colour and remove the lace. The result is always a surprise.
- Thick, fibrous paper can also be very useful (newspaper can do). If a small piece of it is roughly torn across, a jagged edge will be formed. This edge is ideal for creating effects like clouds (overspray white, move the paper to a different angle and repeat), mountain scenery or sea.

French manicure

Airbrushing is a very quick method of applying colour to nails. Some salons have dispensed with traditional nail varnish applications and use their airbrushes entirely.

Examples of airbrushing designs using a variety of techniques

One excellent application is to provide a 'French manicure' for clients by airbrushing the white tip. Stencils are available that concentrate on these shapes. Various-sized curves, for different finger sizes, and other shapes can create the perfect 'French' smile line without the often bulky white varnish that has a tendency to chip.

Like all nail art, its limits are the imagination and airbrush artists who practise are capable of creating stunning and original designs that, of course, can help earn them a good income.

SUMMARY

This final chapter moves from simple nail painting through work with foil, polish secures, glitter, transfers and tape to nail jewellry and advanced airbrushing techniques, where the safety aspects of using the equipment are as important as the actual painting techniques.

Knowledge Reviews

CHAPTER 2

1 Explain eight functions of the skin
2 Name the layers found in the epidermis
3 What are the main structures found in the skin?
4 What part does the matrix play in the process of nail growth?
5 Why is it important to understand the process of nail growth and factors that affect it?
6 Why should special care be taken when working in the area of the lunula?

CHAPTER 3

1 What are the three main artificial nail systems available?
2 Explain: a. vapours, b. fumes, c. odours
3 Ventilation is essential for the safe removal of ……. (a, b or c above)
4 What is the name of the chemical process that changes an artificial nail overlay into a solid?
5 How can room temperature affect artificial nail products?
6 What is the purpose of an initiator in any artificial nail system?
7 Name some problems that could occur as a result of contamination of artificial nail products?

CHAPTER 4

1 Why is it important to have suitable desks and chairs for treatments?
2 How does the Health and Safety at Work Act and the Control of Substances Hazardous to Health Regulations relate to the products being used?
3 What are the main 'routes of entry' of a chemical into the body?
4 How can potentially harmful chemicals be prevented from entering the body?
5 What are the three levels of decontamination?
6 Why is effective decontamination essential before, during and after each treatment?
7 Give one example of the type of products that could be used for each of the levels of decontamination
8 How should solvents be disposed of?

CHAPTER 5

1 What is 'overexposure'?
2 How can overexposure be avoided?
3 Why is effective communication with clients so important at the consultation stage?
4 What treatment alternatives should clients be aware of
5 Why is it important that clients understand all aspects of the treatment, homecare and subsequent treatment requirements?
6 Why are client record cards necessary?
7 Why is safe and effective nail preparation important to a. the health of the natural nail, b. effectiveness of the treatment?
8 How are the correct methods of correct product usage discovered?
9 How would an infection or other contra-indication be recognized?

CHAPTER 6

1 What are the features of a plastic tip?
2 How is a tip type chosen to fit a client's nail?
3 Why is the correct width of tip so important?
4 How can any damage to the natural nail during blending be avoided?
5 How can tips be customized to fit various nail shapes?
6 Ideally what is the maximum length of an artificial nail while still keeping the nail balanced?
7 What would you do if there is a bubble under the tip?

CHAPTER 7

1 Explain briefly the application of: a. powder/liquid, b. UV gel, c. fibre systems
2 What structure creates the maximum strength for a finished nail?
3 What is meant by perfect shape and balance?
4 What is the purpose of zoning?
5 Suggest two methods of application that could correct or improve various nail shapes
6 What conditions could adversely affect the application of overlays?
7 In a UV cured material what inhibits polymerization?
8 Why is it important to provide treatments within commercially acceptable timings?

CHAPTER 8

1 What is the difference between a 'free form' sculptured nail and a tip with overlay?
2 Why do many forms have a metallic finish?
3 Why is zoning especially important in a sculptured nail?
4 When applying a form, what are the two curves that must be followed?

CHAPTER 9

1 How is the structure of the artificial nail affected after 2–3 weeks' growth?

2 What is the difference between an infill and a rebalance treatment?

3 Why is it important that clients return for regular maintenance treatments?

4 Name four reasons for the overlay to lift in Zone 3

5 Why is effective communication important during maintenance treatments?

6 Why is homecare advice essential and what are the main points to be covered?

7 What would you do if discoloration was noticed under the overlay?

Glossary of
Terms

This glossary of terms relates to the words shown in **bold** in the book on their first use and the context in which they have been used. Many of the words have several meanings. Other definitions can be found in a dictionary or encyclopedia.

Abrasive   Material used to shape, polish and remove the surface of natural and artificial nails

ABS   Acrylonitrile-butadiene-styrene; a polymer from which most plastic tips are made

Absorption   In this context, one of the nail 'routes of entry' into the body; that is, through the skin

Acetone   A solvent. Commonly used as a tip remover and nail varnish remover

Acids   Substances that have pH values of less than 7.0; the opposite of **alkaline**

Acid mantle   A mixture of sweat and sebum on the skin that has a pH value of 5.5 and acts as a protection against bacteria

Acrylates   A 'family' of organic chemicals

Acrylics   In this context, 'systems' that use two components, liquid monomer and powder polymer, to create an artificial overlay

Activator   One of the components in the 'fibre system'; this is a liquid that speeds up the polymerization of a cyanoacrylate resin

Adhesion   A force that makes two surfaces stick together

Adhesives   Chemicals that cause two surfaces to stick together; the most common adhesive in the nail industry is cyanoacrylate

AHA   Alpha hydroxy acid. Relatively mild fruit acid used as an ingredient in some skin care products. They can assist exfoliation and encourage healthy cell renewal

Albinism   A skin condition where the skin cells do not produce any melanin

Alkaline   The opposite of acid. 7–14 in the pH scale

Allergic reaction   The reaction of the body to an invasion of a chemical substance or foreign body that could be harmful or that the body has developed a sensitivity to. Can be topical (restricted to an area) or systemic (affects the whole body)

Allergen   A substance that causes an allergy

Amine   A type of chemical compound

Amino acids   Small molecules that the body uses as building blocks for proteins

Antiseptic   A sanitizer, the lowest level of decontamination, usually suitable for skin use

Apocrine gland   One of the two types of gland found in the skin. This one is only found in the armpit and groin area and is controlled by hormones

Arteries   Blood vessels that carry the blood from the heart to other parts of the body

Atom   Smallest unit of matter that is recognisable as a chemical

Bacteria   A single-cell, vegetable-like organism; some are capable of causing disease

Beau's lines   Horizontal lines on nail plate

Benzoyl peroxide   A heat-sensitive catalyst often found in powder polymers

Blue nails   A condition usually associated with circulation problems where the nail bed appears blue rather than pink

Brittleness   The condition of a substance that determines how likely it is to break

Bruised nails   An area of skin beneath the nail that has suffered some form of trauma causing blood from local vessels to leak into surrounding tissues

'C' curve   The curve of the nail from side wall to side wall

Capillaries   The smallest blood vessels that carry blood to all parts of the body

Catalyst   A chemical added to a substance to promote, speed or control the chemical reaction or polymerization; a catalyst does not take part in the chemical reaction

Cell   The smallest unit capable of life

Chemicals   Matter; everything except light and electricity is a chemical

Chemical bond   The bonds between the atoms and molecules of a chemical

Chemical reaction   A process of two or more chemicals combining to create a different substance

Collagen   Fibre proteins found in the skin that help provide support to the structure of the skin and surrounding tissues

Contamination   Unwanted or foreign substances on an implement, surface or in a product

Copolymer   A polymer made from two or more different monomers

Corrosive   Substances capable of causing rapid and sometimes irreversible damage to human tissue or other surfaces

Cross-links   Chemical bonds between polymer chains

Cross-linker   A monomer that links chains of polymers together

Cure   Polymerization

Curing   The process of polymerization

Cuticle   A very thin layer of skin growing from under the lateral nail fold that adheres to the nail plate

Cyanoacrylates   The family of acrylates used in adhesives and resins

Cytoplasm   The gel-like contents of a living cell that contains the cellular structures

Decontamination   The process of reducing the risk of harm from pathogenic micro-organisms

Dehydrate   To remove water from the surface of the natural nail plate

Dermatitis   Non-specific skin inflammation

Dermis   Lower layer of skin, below the epidermis

Desquamation   The shedding of non living cells

Disinfectant   Substance capable of killing some micro-organisms and inhibiting the growth of others; second level of decontamination

Disinfection   A level of decontamination that kills some living organisms and inhibits the growth of others. Suitable for hard surfaces and implements.

Distal   Refers to the part of a structure that is furthest from the centre of the body

Distal nail plate   The part of the nail plate at the end of the finger; free edge

Eccrine glands   One of the two types of gland found in the skin. Found all over the body except in the armpit and groin. Helps eliminate waste products and control body temperature.

Eggshell nails   Thin delicate nails, usually curving under at the free edge

Elastin   Fibre of protein found in the skin that helps the skin maintain its elastic properties and return to shape

Elements   The smallest part of a chemical that can recognizably exist

Epidermis   Upper layer of skin, above the dermis

Eponychium   The skin fold and seal that is at the base of the nail plate

Ethyl cyanoacrylate   One of the acrylate-based family of adhesives, usually used as a nail adhesive

Ethyl methacrylate (EMA)   A monomer most commonly used in acrylic nail systems

Evaporation   The conversion of a liquid into a vapour

Exothermic   Heat-producing chemical reaction

Extensions   Artificially extending the length of a fingernail

Fabric mesh   Usually a silk or fibreglass fabric used in a fabric 'system' to provide extra strength

Fan-shaped nail   A nail plate that is wider at the free edge than at the cuticle

Fibre   In this context, the 'system' that uses a fibre (e.g. silk, fibreglass) with a cyanoacrylate resin to create an artificial overlay

Fibreglass   A fine mesh of fibreglass used to strengthen a cyanoacrylate resin system

Flexibility   The property of a substance that determines how much it will bend

Follicles   Found in the skin; the hair follicle is where the hair is formed

Free edge   The part of the nail plate that extends past the end of the finger

French manicure   A method of painting nails using a white colour on the free edge and a transparent natural colour over the nail bed

Fumes   Particles suspended in smoke

Fungus (fungi)   Microscopic plant; can colonize or grow on or under the nail plate and skin, and can lead to medical problems

Furrows   Longitudinal ridges on the nail plate

Gel   Thickened liquids; can refer to a thick adhesive or a UV-cured material

Gel stage   Refers to the start of the polymerization process of an 'acrylic' system when the liquid and powder react forming a 'gel-like' substance before hardening or curing

Glues   Often used to describe adhesives; its true meaning is an adhesive that is protein-based, usually animal-derived (e.g. bones, hides, etc.)

Grit   Used to describe the abrasiveness of files and buffers; the higher the number, the finer the abrasive – a level of not less than 240 grit should be used on the natural nail

Habit tic   An habitual action that damages the matrix of a nail. Usually seen on the thumb where the forefinger picks at the nail fold

Hangnail   Sharp piece of nail in the side walls that is separated from the nail plate

Hardness   A measure of how easily a substance can be scratched

Hazardous ingredients   Substances that may be capable of causing physical or health-related injury

Histamine   A chemical released by the body as a defence mechanism to protect against harm from an unwanted substance that causes an irritation or other type of reaction

Hooked (or claw) nail   A nail plate that has an extreme upper arch and curves under at the free edge (claw nail)

Hyponychium   The distal edge of the nail bed; a seal between the nail plate and nail bed

Infill   A treatment than compensates for the natural nail growth after the application of artificial nails. Usually 2–3 weeks after application

Ingestion   One of the main 'routes of entry' into the body; that is, via the mouth

Inhalation   One of the main 'routes of entry' into the body; that is, via the lungs

Initiator   A chemical that starts the chemical process of polymerization

Irritants   Substances capable of causing inflammation of the skin, eyes, nose, throat or lungs

Irritation   A general description of a mildly inflammatory condition

Keratin   A protein created by the body and one that is formed when skin cells have become keratinized to form the nail plate

Keratinised   The description of a skin or nail cell that has lost its contents and transformed into the protein keratin

Koilonychia   Flat, spoon-shaped nails usually with a systemic cause

Lamellar dystrophy   Peeling, splitting layers of the nail plate

Lateral   To the side

Leucoderma   Patches of skin that do not have any pigmentation

Leukonychia   White spots on the nail plate; usually caused by trauma to the nail plate but may have other medical causes

Lateral nail fold   Skin on either side of the nail plate

Lifting   Term used to describe the separation of an artificial nail overlay from the nail plate

Light cured   The process of polymerization using a photoinitiator to start the chemical reaction, usually UV light

Lipid   A natural fat produced by the skin; this helps to form part of the intercellular cement that holds keratinized skin cells together

Liquid   The most common definition is a physical state, e.g. solid, gas, liquid; in the context of nail products, it refers to the monomer in a two-component acrylic system

Low odour   Sometimes used in the context of acrylic monomers; means that they have a lower evaporation rate or are not so easily detected by the human sense of smell; does not refer to degree of safety

Lower arch   The curve of the lower part of the free edge when viewed from the side

Lunula   Whitish area at the base of the nail plate where keratinization is incomplete; often referred to the 'half moon'

Lymph   A clear fluid circulating the body via the lymphatic system whose main functions are to fight infection and remove waste

Mantle   The area of skin that covers the matrix; proximal nail fold

Matrix   Area below the proximal nail fold where the process of keratinization of skin cells takes place to form the nail plate

Melanin   A pigment created by specialist skin cells to protect the lower layers of skin from sun damage

Melanocytes   Adapted skin cells that produce the pigment melanin

Methacrylic acid   An acid commonly used as a primer in many nail systems

Methyl methacrylate (MMA)   A monomer no longer used as a component of an acrylic system except as a 'co-polymer' with ethyl methacrylate (EMA)

Mist   Fine liquid particles produced by spraying

Mitosis   The process of cell division and reproduction

Molecule   A specific arrangement of atoms to create a specific chemical

Monomer   One unit or molecule; individual chemical units that can react to form a polymer

Mould   A term often and incorrectly used to describe nail infections, usually pseudomonas (green infection between the nail plate and overlay)

MSDS   Material Safety Data Sheet; forms that provide various information relating to safety issues

Nail bed   Area of skin that lies directly under the nail plate

Nail enamel   A term sometimes used to describe a product used to apply colour to the nails

Nail lacquer   See **Nail enamel**

Nail plate   The hard layers of keratinized skin cells that form a 'plate' on the end of each finger and toe

Nail polish   See **Nail enamel**

Nail unit   The area at the end of the finger that includes all parts of the finger nail

Nail varnish   See **Nail enamel**

Nail wraps   Most commonly, a fibre system used to overlay the natural nail; can refer to any system.

National Occupational Standards   The level and detail of the various competencies required by specific industry sectors that make a person capable of carrying out specific work, laid down by the industry sector.

Natural nail   The fingernail that is formed in the matrix to make a nail plate

Natural nail overlays   Artificial nail products used to coat a natural nail plate

No-light gel   A cyanoacrylate-based gel

Non-acetone polish remover   Solvents for polish removal, usually recommended for use with artificial nails; however, all solvents can damage some artificial nails

NVQ   National Vocational Qualification; a qualification based on the National Occupational Standards and strongly promoted by Department for Education and Employment

Odour   Presence of a chemical that can be detected by the sense of smell. Is not an indication of degree of danger or quantity of chemical

Oligomers   Chains of monomers that are considerably shorter than a polymer

Onychocryptosis   Ingrowing nail

Onychodermal band   Seal between the nail plate and the hyponychium

Onycholysis   Separation of the natural nail from the nail bed

Onychomadesis   Loosening of the nail plate at the proximal nail fold; usually due to trauma

Onychomycosis   Lifting, discoloured or rotting of the nail plate

Onychophagy The habit of nail biting

Onychorrhexis Longitudinal splitting of the nail plate; often associated with furrows

Optical brightener A additive that makes colours look brighter and white look whiter

Organic Any substance that contains the element carbon; it does not relate to the degree of safety: virtually every product used in the nail industry is organic

Overlay A coating applied to the natural nail or blended plastic tip and natural nail

Paronychia Inflammation caused by damage of foreign body around the edges of the nail plate

Pathogen A micro-organism capable of causing disease

pH value A measure used to determine the level of acidity or alkalinity of a substance; 7 is neutral, 1 is the most acidic and 14 is the most alkaline

Photoinitiator A chemical that responds to specific types of light to start a chemical reaction

Pitting A description of the surface of the nail plate that has small dips in it. Often a sign of a skin condition such as psoriasis

Plasticizer An additive that increases flexibility

Polish remover Solvents that remove polish from the nail

Polymers Literally 'many units'; very long chains of chemically bonded monomers or units

It can refer to the acrylics used in artificial nails; it also refers to any other polymer, e.g. hair, that is chains of amino acids

Polymerization A chemical reaction that creates polymer chains from monomers or oligomers

Ppm Parts per million; a general measure of ratio; in this context, it can be the number of molecules of vapour in 1 million molecules of air

Powder Materials that have been finely ground; in this context, powder generally refers to powder polymers which are tiny beads of a polymer

Pretailor To shape a plastic tip before application to create a better fit and shape

Primer A substance used to improve the adhesion between the nail plate and artificial products

Protein Chemical substances created by the body from long chains of amino acids

Proximal Nearest to the centre of the body

Proximal nail fold The fold of epidermis covering the matrix and extending onto the nail plate

Psoriasis A non contagious skin condition

Resin Refers to a version of cyanoacrylate used in the fibre system

Resin activator A product that speed up the cure time of a cyanoacrylate resin

Risk assessment A requirement of COSHH that assesses potential hazards

Routes of entry   The three ways a chemical can enter the body: ingestion (mouth), inhalation (nose), absorption (skin)

Sanitization   To kill or reduce the numbers of pathogens to a level considered safe by public health standards

Sculptured nails   Artificial nails created by building the nail onto the natural nail and extending it over a form rather than a plastic tip

Sebum   A natural oil produced by the sebaceous glands attached to hair follicles that moisturizes and lubricates the skin and plays a protective role

Sensitization   The biological process of becoming sensitive to a chemical that usually results in an allergic reaction

Side wall   The soft tissue along the sides of the nail plate

Ski-jump nail   A nail plate that curves upwards from the cuticle area to the free edge

Smile line   The curve that's created naturally by the hyponychium or by a coloured artificial overlay or nail varnish

Solehorn   Epidermis attached to the underside of some natural nails; more often seen on nails that are almond shaped: it has a blood and nerve supply, so should not be removed

Solvents   Substances capable of dissolving other substances; water is the 'universal solvent'

Splinter haemorrhage   Small black streaks under the nail plate

Sterilization   The process that achieves the complete destruction of all living organisms

Stop point   The part of a plastic tip that fits around the free edge of the natural nail

Stratum corneum   Uppermost layer of the epidermis consisting of keratinised skin cells

Stratum germinativum   Base layer of the epidermis where new skin cells are formed

Stratum granulosm   One of the mid layers of the epidermis where the process of keratinisation starts

Stratum lucidium   One of the mid layers of the epidermis apparent in the palms of the hands and soles of the feet

Stratum spinosum   One of the mid layers of the epidermis where some cells are connected together

Strength   The ability of a substance to withstand breakage if force is applied

Subcutaneous layer   Below the dermis of the skin where fat is stored

Sun damage   Damage to the skin where the skin has created permanent melanin discolouration, e.g. freckles

Sweat   A liquid produced by the sweat glands in the skin; one of the main functions of sweat is to help regulate body temperature

System   In this context, this refers to the 'system' used to overlay the natural nail or plastic tip, e.g. acrylic, UV gel

Thixotropic   The ability of a liquid to become thinner in viscosity when agitated, returning to its original viscosity when agitation stops

Titanium dioxide   A white pigment used in white-tip powders

Toxic   The description of a substance that can adversely harm humans at measured levels

True cuticle   The layer of skin that is continuously shed from the underside of the proximal nail fold and adheres to the nail plate

Ultraviolet (UV) light   An invisible part of the spectrum above the colour violet in the visible light bands

Upper arch   The curve of the nail from the cuticle area to the free edge

UV absorbers   Additives that act like sunscreens

UV block   A chemical ingredient that prevents UV rays from affecting the product or underlying skin tissues

UV gel   One of the 'systems' of artificial nails; it uses a premixed 'gel' and UV light to create the overlay

Vapours   Molecules of a chemical in air created by evaporation of the substance

Ventilation   The process of changing the air in an area and therefore removing dust and vapours

Viruses   A wide group of micro-organisms that can only reproduce in living cells and can cause a vast range of disease

Viscosity   The measure of a liquid's ability to flow, that is, its thinness or thickness

Vitamin D   A vitamin formed in the body and essential for the efficient absorption and use of calcium

Vitiligo   A condition of the skin where it is not able to produce the pigment melanin

Volatile   Describes a substance that easily evaporates in air

Warts   Lumps of usually hard tissue on the skin caused by a viral infection

Wetting   The ability of a liquid to spread out to cover a surface

White-tip powder   A colour of acrylic powder used to create a white free edge on an artificial nail

Whitlow   Localized and painful swelling at the edge of the nail plate

Yeast   A type of fungus; some yeasts can cause fungal infections

Zones   The three areas of the artificial nail referred to when creating the correct artificial structure